THEMATIC UNIT

U.S. CONSTITUTION

Written by Mary Ellen Sterling

Illustrated by Janet Armbrust

Teacher Created Materials, Inc.
P.O. Box 1040
Huntington Beach, CA 92647
© *1993 Teacher Created Materials, Inc.*
Made in U.S.A.
ISBN 1-55734-582-1

Table of Contents

Introduction

U.S. Constitution contains a captivating, whole language thematic unit about the writing of the United States Constitution. Its eighty exciting pages are filled with a wide variety of lesson ideas and reproducible pages designed for use at the challenging level. At its core are three high-quality children's literature selections, *Shh! We're Writing the Constitution, We the People,* and *The Great Little Madison.* The first selection introduces the background and story of the writing of the Constitution while the second literature piece deals with the actual contents of the document. *The Great Little Madison* goes beyond the constitutional story and explores the life of one of the men who was most responsible for its existence, James Madison, our fourth President.

There are activites included for each selection which set the stage for reading, encourage enjoyment of the book, and extend the concepts. In addition, the theme is connected to the curriculum with activities in language arts, daily writing assignments, math, science, social studies, art, music, and life skills. Many of these activities encourage cooperative learning. The majority of them were planned with the idea of interrelationship. Many overlap each story and can be used with any of the selections.

Challenging thematic units should be planned with an understanding of the reading levels and organizational abilities of the individuals and unique groups that will be participating in the unit. Some classes will take more time to cover the unit, while others will be able to do more projects independently or in cooperative learning groups.

This thematic unit includes:

- **literature selections**—summaries of three books with related lessons that cross the curriculum

- **planning guides**— suggestions for sequencing lessons each day of the unit

- **poetry**—suggested selections and lessons enabling students to write their own works

- **writing ideas**—writing activities across the curriculum

- **bulletin board ideas**—suggestions and plans for student-created bulletin boards

- **curriculum connections**—in language arts, math, science, social studies, art, music, and life skills

- **group projects**—to foster cooperative learning

- **culminating activities**—which require students to synthesize their learning and produce products that can be shared with others

- **a bibliography**—suggesting additional literature and nonfiction books on the theme

> To keep this valuable resource intact so that it can be used year after year, you may wish to punch holes in the pages and store them in a three-ring binder.

Introduction *(cont.)*

Why Whole Language?

A whole language approach involves children in using all modes of communication: reading, writing, listening, observing, illustrating, experiencing, and doing. Communication skills are interconnected and integrated into lessons that emphasize the whole of language rather than isolating its parts. The lessons revolve around the selected literature. Reading is not taught as a separate subject from writing and spelling, for example. A child reads, writes, speaks, listens, etc., in response to a literature experience introduced by the teacher. In this way, language skills grow naturally, stimulated by involvement and interest in the topic at hand.

Why Thematic Planning?

One very useful tool for implementing an integrated whole language program is thematic planning. By choosing a theme with correlating literature selections for a unit of study, a teacher can plan activities throughout a day that lead to a cohesive, in-depth study of the topic. Students will be practicing and applying their skills in meaningful contexts. Consequently, they will tend to learn and retain more. Both teachers and students will be freed from a day that is broken into unrelated segments of isolated drill and practice.

Why Cooperative Learning?

Along with academic skills and content, students need to learn social skills. No longer can this area of development be taken for granted. Students must learn to work cooperatively in groups in order to function well in modern society. Group activities should be a regular part of school life and teachers should consciously include social objectives as well as academic objectives in their planning. For example, a group working together to write a play may need to select a leader. The teacher should make clear to the students and monitor the qualities of good leader-follower group interaction just as he/she would state and monitor the academic goals of the project.

4

Shh! We're Writing the Constitution

by Jean Fritz

Summary

When the thirteen colonies ratified the Declaration of Independence on July 4, 1776, they agreed to retain their own sovereignty. While they were glad they were no longer under British rule, they were not yet ready to call themselves Americans. The states enjoyed having their own character and the freedom to make their own decisions. As time progressed, however, it became clear that if they were to survive as a nation they would need some kind of united government. The Continental Congress, which had previously been established, was weak and limited in its powers. It could declare war, but the individual states weren't obligated to supply soldiers. Laws could be passed, but there was no way to enforce them. In addition, states began to fight among themselves over water use rights and tariffs. Clearly, something would have to be done.

In 1786 George Washington, Alexander Hamilton, and James Madison suggested to the Continental Congress the possibility of a Grand Convention. Each state would send delegates to this meeting for the purpose of improving the existing form of government. Some states balked at the suggestion and refused to attend while others embraced the idea whole-heartedly. *Shh! We're Writing the Constitution* is the story of what happened during the proceedings of these historic meetings. Despite its shaky start and the often disagreeable circumstances in which its members had to work, the convention managed to put together one of the most important documents ever written. Once again Jean Fritz has made history come alive with her engaging writing style. Students will find this book interesting to read and will also be able to use it for reference since the Constitution is printed in the last pages of the book.

Sample Plan

Lesson 1

- Prepare a bulletin board. (See page 77 for ideas).
- Set the stage. Cover the windows. (See #1, p. 6).
- Brainstorm. Make a chart of living conditions in the 1700s.
- Vocabulary. Copy words onto board; define.

Lesson 2

- Read the book.
- Vocabulary. Find the words in context.
- Daily writing. Use the topics on page 12.
- Simulation. Do activity #3 on page 15.
- Science. Choose from activities on page 23.

Lesson 3

- Expand Vocabulary (oral activity, page 11).
- Continue daily writing (topics, page 12).
- Make hornbooks, quills, parchment. (See page 8.)

- They Were There (worksheet, page 14).
- Begin comprehension questions, page 17.

Lesson 4

- Continue daily writing (topics, page 12).
- Expand vocabulary words with probing questions (#4, page 10).
- Math (Facts and Figures, page 16).
- Continue comprehension questions, page 17.
- Art (Silhouettes page 22).

Lesson 5

- Test comprehension with The Constitutional Story, page 19.
- Write new lyrics for 1700s songs (page 21).
- Meet the author, Jean Fritz (page 24).

Overview of Activities

Setting the Stage

1. Cover the windows with butcher paper or newspaper before the students come into the classroom. Light a candle and leave the lights off. Read aloud an excerpt from *Shh! We're Writing the Constitution*. Discuss the meaning of the passage with the students. Tell them that they are going to be studying in detail the history of how this document originated.

2. Brainstorm with the students and make a chart of living conditions in the late 1700s. Have them tell what they think schools were like then. Recreate some of those experiences. Students can make a hornbook, a quill, and parchment to use in their daily lessons. Candles can be used to help set the mood during some simulation activities found on page 15. Directions for creating these projects appear on pages 8 and 9.

3. Write the vocabulary words from page 10 onto the board for the students to copy. Tell them to define each word and write each in a complete sentence that makes sense. Save these papers for use while reading *Shh! We're Writing the Constitution*.

Enjoying the Book

1. **Reading the Book.** Assign students to read *Shh! We're Writing the Constitution*. If possible, provide one copy for each group of students.

2. **Vocabulary.** As students read the book, have them find the vocabulary words in the context. Instruct them to copy the whole sentence in which the word appears. Review the meaning of the words as a class. Other activities to build vocabulary appear on page 10.

3. **In the Constitution**. Expand vocabulary and word skills with this whole class activity (page 11). Write the word *constitution* on the chalkboard and explain the directions to the students. Read aloud the clues and call on students to answer or have them write answers on a sheet of paper. Correct the answers as a class.

4. **Creative Writing Topics.** Eight different writing activities can be found on page 12. Employ them throughout the unit wherever they are most appropriate.

5. **Hornbook Pattern.** The simple pattern on page 13 can be used for a variety of projects including creative writing, stationery, handwriting, art lessons, and the construction of bulletin boards. Some sample ideas are outlined on that page. When using the pattern for some activities such as handwriting, you will want to cover up the text before making copies of the hornbook.

6. **They Were There.** Some research may be required to complete the worksheet on page 14. Extend the page by directing the students to write a characterization of another Constitutional figure.

7. **Simulations.** The simulations on page 15 will help students get into the spirit of the times. (For other ideas see Teacher Created Materials #480 - *American History Simulations*.)

Overview of Activities *(cont.)*

Enjoying the Book

8. **Math.** Review Constitutional facts and practice simple computational skills with the worksheet, Facts and Figures, on page 16. Present it as an oral lesson, if you prefer. For more math-related ideas see Constitutional Figures on page 69. It contains a number of creative ways to incorporate math into your unit studies.

9. **Review Comprehension.** Find out how well students retained and understood what they read with the questions on page 17. Suggested ways to use the page are given.

10. **Comprehension Worksheet.** Let students work on their own to complete this review of the Constitutional Story (page 19). A second worksheet on page 20, Constitutional Fill-In, may be used in conjunction with this activity.

Extending the Book

1. **Writing Lyrics.** Learn the words and melodies of some of the songs of the era like "Yankee Doodle," "The Dying British Sergeant," or "God Save the King." Group the students and assign them to write another verse for one of the songs. Have them perform the new lyrics for the whole class. (See page 21 for a prepared worksheet.)

2. **Studying the Newspaper.** Continue to learn about Constitutional times through the daily newspaper. Ask students to bring in articles that show the Constitution in action. For example, they might share an article about a case that has been dismissed because the accused's house was searched illegally. Make a bulletin board display of these articles. In addition, find out if the local newspaper features a daily almanac column. Students will be able to read about events from long ago. Have them write their own statements that begin, "On this day in 1787,..."

3. **Art.** Choose from three projects that are presented on page 22. Display the finished artwork on a bulletin board or at a special center set up in the classroom.

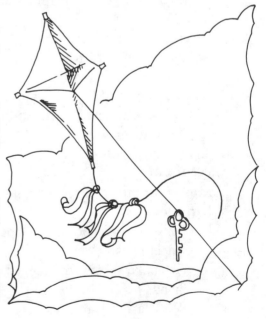

4. **Science.** Direct the students to find out about Benjamin Franklin's famous kite experiment. Extend the research with some experiments on other forms of static electricity. See page 23 for three electrifying activities.

5. **Learn About the Author.** Find out some interesting facts about Jean Fritz. See page 24 for more information and activities.

6. **The Amendments.** Learn about the Constitution and its amendments. (For complete lesson plans see pages 25 to 40.)

7

Re-creating Constitutional Times

The year 1787 is so long ago that students may have difficulty imagining what living conditions might have been like then. Re-creations such as the projects outlined below will help students get into the spirit of the times. Use those that are most appropriate for your class and modify any of the activities to better suit your needs.

1. **Schooling.** Establish that students in 1787 attended one-room schools in which all grades were taught. Lessons were written with a quill on parchment, and the alphabet was learned with the help of a hornbook. Students can make their own hornbook, quill, and parchment by following these directions.

Hornbooks

Materials: pattern from page 13, scissors, glue, cardboard (from a cereal box, etc.), black marking pen

Directions:
- Make copies of the pattern on page 13; give one to each student.
- Have students cut out the hornbook and glue to a piece of cardboard; let dry.
- Students then cut the cardboard to the shape of the hornbook. With a black marking pen, have them write the letters of the alphabet and numerals as shown.

Quills

Materials: wing feather from a turkey, crow, seagull, or goose; sharp knife; pencil; liquid ink

Directions:
- With the knife make an angled cut on the underside of the wing tip (diagram 1).
- Cut the tip square (diagram 2).
- Slit the tip just a little (diagram 3) and press open with a pencil (diagram 4).

Parchment

Materials: brown paper shopping bags, scissors

Directions:
- With the scissors, cut open the brown paper bags.
- To make sheets with ragged edges, tear by hand.
- With a quill and ink, copy the alphabet from the hornbook onto the "parchment."

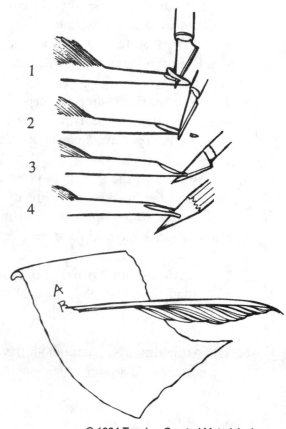

8

Re-creating Constitutional Times *(cont.)*

2. **Lighting.** Although Benjamin Franklin discovered electricity during this time, it would be many years before it would be available to every home as it is today. Back then, people relied on candles and lanterns for lighting purposes. Let the students make their own candles. Cover the class windows, turn out the lights, and do lessons by candlelight.

Candles

Materials: clean empty cardboard juice cans or pint-sized milk cartons, paraffin wax, old candles, small birthday candles, cooking oil, wooden spoon, old pan half full of water, old coffeepot or other spouted can, newspaper

Directions:
- CAUTION! Monitor the temperature of the melting wax carefully. Make sure it does not boil. Just in case the wax should ignite, have sand or baking soda on hand to extinguish the flames.
- Place newspapers over the work area (away from stove).
- Spread cooking oil on the inside surface of the cans or cartons.
- Place the spouted can in the pan of water.
- Place the paraffin into the spouted can; turn stove on low heat.
- Break the candle into pieces (minus the wick) and add to the paraffin in the pan.
- Stir constantly until the wax is melted.
- Pour into prepared cans or cartons. (Fill about halfway.)
- Place a birthday candle into the center of the can or carton.
- Allow to set. Carefully peel away the mold.

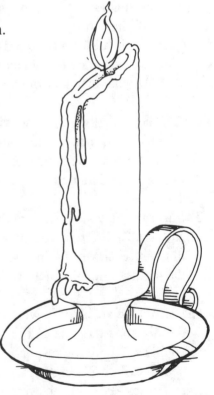

3. **Literature.** Children's literature, as we know it, was nonexistent in the 1700s. Only very wealthy people owned their own books, and libraries were few and far between. To set the mood for this period, read aloud some excerpts from popular literature of the time. Two to choose from are Daniel Defoe's *Robinson Crusoe* and Jonathan Swift's *Gulliver's Travels*.
- Before reading, brainstorm with the students to find out what they know about a title. Record the responses and save for future reference. Add to the list after the reading.
- Have the students draw a picture of what they see when you read the story. Allow students to explain their pictures.
- Find some condensed versions of these two classics for interested students to read.
- Compare the original version of one of these stories to a revised, updated version. Which do students prefer and why?

Building Vocabulary

Listed below are a number of possible vocabulary words taken from the pages of *Shh! We're Writing the Constitution*. Add and/or delete words from the list as you progress through your constitutional unit. Employ any of the activities on this page to help your students build and reinforce their vocabulary knowledge.

sovereign	scoffed	independent	referred
united	allegiance	oath	federation
legislature	delegates	revising	adjourned
sauntered	convention	escorted	sentries
eavesdroppers	document	Constitution	federal
executive	legislative	Congress	representatives
resolutions	revise	aristocratic	monarchy
patriotism	electors	impeach	presiding
measures	bombarded	jeer	droned
stalemate	diversion	legislator	amendments
ratify	Federalist	Nationalist	tyranny
ambassadors	seceding	procession	compromise

Activities

1. Make copies of the vocabulary words in the box above. Group the students and give one copy to each group. Direct the groups to work together to list one of the following:
   a. All the action words
   b. All the descriptive words
   c. All the collective nouns
   d. Another category of their choosing

2. Pair the students for this activity. One partner picks any three vocabulary words and says them aloud to his or her partner. The second partner must use all three words in a sentence which makes sense. Instruct the pairs to change roles and repeat the procedure. Continue as long as student interest is maintained.

3. Illustrate the vocabulary words. Instruct the students to fold a sheet of drawing paper into fourths and write a different vocabulary word at the bottom of each space. Have them draw a picture to illustrate each word. Instead of drawing, students can cut out pictures from magazines to depict the words. Glue the pictures in the proper spaces on the folded sheet of drawing paper.

4. Expand the vocabulary words with probing questions. For example, write the word *document* on the chalkboard or use an overhead projector. Ask the students to tell what kind of document it could be; record the responses on the board or overhead projector. Possible responses include "hand-written," "lengthy," " important," etc. Next, ask where the document might be and record responses. Possible answers include "on a desk," "in his hand," "by the table," etc. Finally, tell the students to write sentences which incorporate some of the phrases they came up with. Share them with a partner.

In the Constitution

On the chalkboard or overhead projector write the word *Constitution*. Explain to students that all the answers to the clues they will be given can be found in the word *Constitution*. For example, the clue is "three of them in an inning." The answer is: "outs." Each letter in the word *outs* can be found in Constitution.

Read each clue aloud. Have all students write an answer on a piece of paper. Call on two students at a time to come to the chalkboard to write a response to the clue. Remind them to use only those letters that appear in the word *Constitution*. **NOTE:** For your reference, answers appear at bottom of page. If reproducing this for student use, fold under directions and answers.

1. _____ a synonym for fat or overweight

2. _____ to name numbers in order

3. _____ metal pieces of money

4. _____ person sent to go in search of something

5. _____ two thousand pounds

6. _____ charges for entry at a college

7. _____ impassive or detached

8. _____ a negative word

9. _____ a kind of collapsible bed

10. _____ involuntary contractions of muscles

11. _____ the son or daughter of your aunt or uncle

12. _____ a type of thread or cloth

13. _____ having to do with the speed of sound

14. _____ a standard basic quantity of measurement

15. _____ a shade or gradation of a color

16. _____ to shock or surprise someone

17. _____ the price charged for something

18. _____ a combination or grouping together

19. _____ hard-shelled fruits such as a pecans

20. _____ a small place of lodging

- -

Answers: 1. stout; 2. count; 3. coins; 4. scout; 5. ton; 6. tuition; 7. stoic; 8. not; 9. cot; 10. tics; 11. cousin; 12. cotton; 13. sonic; 14. unit; 15. tint; 16. stun; 17. cost; 18. union; 19. nuts; 20. inn

Creative Writing Topics

Listed below are a number of suggested writing topics which can be incorporated into a unit of Constitutional studies. Assign a different one each day as a daily writing exercise or give students a choice of two or three of the assignments. Another option is to make copies of this page, cut apart the topics, and distribute. Modify or expand on any topic as necessary.

1. John Dickinson of Delaware wrote many letters home to his four-year-old daughter whom he addressed as "Pa's Precious." Pretend you are Mr. Dickinson. Write a letter home to your daughter explaining the day's proceedings in words she can understand.

2. Only a few delegates, such as Alexander Hamilton, wanted the President to serve a long term. Get into the mind of Alexander Hamilton and write a speech you would give to the Convention to convince them that the presidency should be long-term, possibly for life.

3. At 81 years of age, Benjamin Franklin was the oldest attendee at the Grand Convention. He was in poor health and had to be carried to the meetings in a Chinese sedan chair. In a news feature format, describe Franklin's colorful entry to the meetings.

4. Elbridge Gerry of Massachusetts was labeled a "Grumbletonian" because he always grumbled and complained about things. Make up a nickname for one of the other delegates. Write a story that explains how or why he got his nickname.

5. Choose a section (except section 1) from Article 1 of the Constitution. With a partner rewrite the paragraph using modern terminology. Share your completed work with another student pair.

6. One delegate, Oliver Ellsworth of Connecticut, had interesting news to write home. He had seen an Egyptian mummy that was on display in Philadelphia. Wondering what the flesh was like, he took out a knife and tested it. Write a creative story about what Mr. Ellsworth found when he cut open the mummy.

7. The delegates to the Convention decided to keep the proceedings a secret so that others could not listen in and take sides. Make a list of at least ten things people on the outside might have said when they found out the meetings were not going to be open to the public.

8. Bluebottle flies attacked the delegates as they stepped outside the State House and even invaded bedrooms where they buzzed around all night. Imagine how you would have felt as these flies bombarded you in your sleeping quarters. Write a creative story telling about your adventures with an especially pesky bluebottle fly.

9. Read "The Silent Lobby" by Mildred Pitts Walter (found in *The Big Book for Peace*, edited by Ann Durell and Marilyn Sachs, Dutton Children's Books, 1990). Write a story about voting rights then and now.

Hornbook Pattern

This hornbook pattern has a number of possible applications, some of which are listed below. Before making copies of this page for student use, you may want to cover up the text that appears within this hornbook pattern.

1. **Template.** Make a template of the pattern. Make a copy of this page and cut out around the hornbook. Glue to tagboard or other heavy paper. Cut around the shape and outline it with a wide-line marking pen. Students can use the template to make more shaped pages for a writing or art project.

2. **Simulation.** Students can make a hornbook replica using the pattern on this page as a guide. (See page 15 for further directions.)

3. **Stationery.** Block out the directions on this page before making a copy of the hornbook outline. Make one copy of the page and with a ruler draw some lines. Copy the page again for some hornbook stationery.

4. **Lessons.** Direct the students to make a hornbook using tagboard. Laminate each one or cover with clear, self-sticking paper. Write on the surface with water-based, wipe-off pens. Students can do their daily math lesson or handwriting lesson on the hornbooks.

5. **Creative Writing.** Tell students to make as many hornbook pages as they will need. (Use the template in #1 above or give each student one copy of this page for a pattern.) Assign a creative writing topic. (See page 12 for some suggestions.)

6. **Social Studies.** Research how hornbooks were constructed. Tell students to write the steps or desribe the process. They can use a hornbook shape on which to write this information.

7. **Bulletin Board.** This hornbook pattern can be used in the construction of bulletin boards. (For some ideas see page 77.)

8. **Handwriting.** Direct students to copy the Preamble onto a hornbook pattern. Remind them to use their best handwriting. (For a copy of the Preamble's text see page 28.)

They Were There

In 1787, from mid-May to mid-September, a group of fifty-five delegates met to construct a document which would unify and solidify the government of the thirteen existing colonies. Among this group were lawyers (over half of them) and statesmen. All were well-educated, well-read, and knowledgeable about the modern schools of political philosophy.

Read the characterizations of some of the delegates who participated in the creation of the Constitution of the United States of America. Write the name of the proper delegate in the space provided.

1. _____ This New York lawyer was born and raised in the Caribbean Islands. He was in favor of a strong central government with power to act for all the states.

2. _____ The oldest of the delegates, he experienced so much pain when being bounced about in a carriage that he had to be carried to the proceedings in a sedan chair.

3. _____ For his participation in the fine-tuning and polishing of the final draft of the Constitution, he was given the nickname "the man who wrote the Constitution."

4. _____ Some delegates sent for their families, but others could only write letters home. This Delaware representative wrote to his four-year-old Maria, whom he called "Pa's Precious."

5. _____ In writing the Virginia Plan this governor and his delegation proposed two houses of a national congress, one elected directly by the people and the other by state legislators.

6. _____ Although he was doubtful at first that national unity could be achieved, he played a key role in the convention as its unanimously-elected president.

7. _____ He was small in stature—some say he was "no bigger than a piece of soap"—but large on ambition. This Virginian hand-recorded all that was said throughout the convention.

8. _____ It took historians almost two years to discover the name of the gentleman who had actually penned the Constitution. He was also clerk of the Pennsylvania House of Delegates.

9. _____ Behind his back he was sometimes called "Grumbletonian." This Massachusetts delegate did not back a national government but merely wanted to revise the Articles of Confederation.

10. _____ A long-winded and boring speaker, this Maryland representative repeated himself so much that Madison did not bother to write it all down.

14

Constitutional Era Simulations

Help students capture the spirit of the Constitutional era with these simulation experiences. Although the activities presented here involve the whole class, students may be grouped or paired to complete some tasks.

1. **Class Meeting.** Delegates to the Grand Convention determined that it was necessary to conduct the meetings in private. Windows were covered and sentries were posted at the door. Assign students to cover the classroom windows with newspaper or butcher paper so that others cannot see in. Post two guards by the classroom door to keep anyone from entering the room. Conduct a whole class meeting in which the students choose a president to lead their meeting. Discuss the comprehension questions from page 17. Afterwards, talk about the experience and how the students felt about sealing off the classroom.

2. **Alternate Meeting.** Keep the classroom windows covered for this activity. With the whole group, brainstorm a list of classroom rules that they would like to have in effect. For example, allowing gum-chewing to be permissible at all times. Record the rules on chart paper or the chalkboard. Next, divide half the students into pairs and make the others one large group. Allow each group the same number of votes as there are members. For example, a pair gets two votes while a group of ten gets ten votes. Have the students vote on the various rules and then discuss the fairness of the voting. How would they change the system so that small groups were represented more fairly? Do students see any similarities between this situation and the one that confronted the states before the Great Compromise was reached?

3. **A Great Compromise.** Divide the class into groups of various sizes. You might have pairs of students; groups of three, four, or five; and a group of seven or more. Supply each group with a stack of index cards or pre-cut construction paper. Write a list of vocabulary words on the chalkboard or overhead projector for all to see. Tell students that they will be making flashcards by writing one word on each index card. Their goal is to make as many cards as possible, and the group with the most cards after a two-minute timed session will win a prize. Have them begin and end on a given signal. Follow up this project with a discussion of whether or not it was a fair assignment. What would have made it more fair? Relate this exercise to the dilemma faced by the Grand Convention in making sure that all states were represented more equally.

4. **Keeping the Minutes.** From the opening to the closing of the meetings of the states' delegates, James Madison kept a written record of the proceedings. His task would have been much easier if tape recorders or video recorders had been available. Writing tools were crude and included liquid ink and quill pens made of feathers. Give students an idea of how difficult Madison's job was by directing them to make their own quills (page 8) and to use the quills to take down notes as you dictate a story to them. See the Bibliography on page 79 for some possible titles.

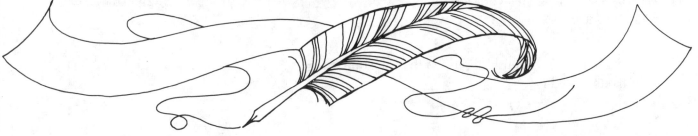

Facts and Figures

Test your knowledge of facts and figures with the problems on this page. Write the correct numbers in the spaces provided. Then perform the function indicated to find an answer. Write answers in the correct spaces.

1. The total number of delegates _____ x the number of states _____ = _____.

2. The year when the Grand Convention began _____ + the year the Articles of Confederation were adopted _____ = _____.

3. The number of articles in the Constitution _____ x Ben Franklin's age at that time _____ = _____.

4. The year the First Continental Congress met _____ ÷ the number of houses in the legislature _____ = _____.

5. The year that New Jersey ratified the Constitution _____ – the year the Declaration of Independence passed _____ = _____.

6. The year North Carolina signed the Constitution _____ x the number of years of a President's term _____ = _____.

7. The number of years a senator is required to be a citizen _____ x William Paterson's height in inches _____ = _____.

8. The year Rhode Island signed the Constitution _____ ÷ by the number of amendments in the Bill of Rights _____ = _____.

9. The number of people at Philadelphia's 4th of July celebration _____ – the number of people who marched in the parade _____ = _____.

10. The year in which Georgia ratified the Constitution _____ x the number of branches of government _____ = _____.

11. The year the Grand Convention was suggested _____ + the year the North agreed to continue slave trade _____ = _____.

12. The year that New Hampshire ratified the Constitution _____ – the day in April that Maryland ratified it _____ = _____.

16

Conventional Comprehension Questions

Develop the critical thinking skill of comprehension with the questions on this page. (Possible answers appear on page 18.) Modify the following four assignments to suit your classroom needs.

- Write one question on the board each day. Direct the students to copy the question and to write an answer. Use as a daily writing activity. At day's end, take some time to let some students share their answers.

- Use these questions for whole class discusssions. (See the simulation activity on page 15.)

- Present these questions as a written assignment. Provide each student with a copy of the page or make a transparency of the questions for use on an overhead projector.

- Direct the students to copy each question on a separate page of a composition book or notebook. Have them write answers to the questions. Students can use the books as a study guide. Create an evaluation tool based on these questions and answers.

QUESTIONS

1. Why did George Washington scoff at the idea of "sovereign states"?
2. What were the Articles of Confederation?
3. Why did the Articles of Confederation not work?
4. What was the original purpose of the Grand Convention?
5. Why did the first meeting not begin on May 14, 1781, as planned?
6. Why was it decided to keep the meetings secret?
7. What provisions were in Governor Randolph's Virginia Plan?
8. Why did the smaller states fear the larger states?
9. What were the terms of the presidency that were finally reached?
10. What did the people of Philadelphia do to keep the delegates happy?
11. What were some of the hardships faced by the delegates?
12. What were the terms of the Great Compromise?
13. What bargain did the North and South strike on the issue of slavery?
14. What were the citizenship requirements for legislators and the President?
15. What was Madison's position about a Bill of Rights?
16. Who were the Federalists? the Anti-Federalists?
17. What is the system of Checks and Balances?
18. Who approves the President's choices for Supreme Court judges and other offices?
19. Why can it be said that the people themselves had the controlling power?
20. Which state was the first to ratify the Constitution? the last?
21. What nickname was given to the Constitution?
22. Where were John Adams and Thomas Jefferson during the Constitutional proceedings?

Answers to Comprehension Questions

Possible answers to the questions from page 17 appear below. You may want students to expand on them.

1. Because he knew that the states could not be truly independent for long and still survive.
2. A list of rules for a "firm league of friendship" among the states.
3. Although Congress could make all the rules it wanted, there was no real way to enforce them.
4. To improve the existing form of government by revising the old Articles of Confederation.
5. Only delegates from two states showed up that day; representatives from seven states were needed to begin proceedings.
6. The delegates did not want the whole country to listen in and take sides.
7. There would be three branches of government—executive, legislative, and judicial. The legislative branch would consist of two houses—the House of Representatives and the Senate.
8. Because the larger states had more people. In the past, votes of all states—no matter what the population—had counted the same. This new government was as much concerned with individuals as with the states.
9. There would be a single executive who would be paid out of the treasury of the new government. He would be chosen by electors from each state and serve a term of four years. If necessary, he could be impeached.
10. Entertained them, provided musicals, covered the cobblestone with gravel to make it quieter.
11. They were away from their families; the heat; bluebottle flies; prisoners jeered at them; long-winded speeches from other delegates.
12. Every state would have two members in the Senate and be allowed two votes; the House of Representatives would have one representative for every 40,000 inhabitants.
13. Northern states agreed to continue the slave trade until 1808, while the Southern states gave up their demand that commercial regulations had to be passed by a two-thirds vote of both Houses.
14. Senators have to be citizens for nine years, representatives for seven, and the President must be native born.
15. He felt it was taken for granted that individuals kept all the rights that they did not specifically give over to the government.
16. Federalists were those people who were for the Constitution; Anti-Federalists were against it.
17. Every bill the House passed had to go to the Senate for approval. If it made it through the Senate, it went to the President for his signature. If he did not like the bill, he could veto it. However, the bill could pass anyway if two-thirds of the House and Senate voted for it. Finally, the Supreme Court could determine if a law was constitutional or not.
18. The Senate.
19. Every four years they would be electing a President; at stated intervals they would elect representatives to Congress.
20. Delaware was first; Rhode Island was last.
21. "The Supreme Law of the land."
22. John Adams was serving as an ambassador to England; Thomas Jefferson was serving as ambassador to France.

18

Constitutional Story

Read the story below. Fill in the blanks with words found in the text of *Shh! We're Writing the Constitution*. Then write the words in the proper spaces of the Constitutional Fill-In on page 20.

After the Revolutionary War, the 1._____ was instituted by the thirteen

states. Each state 2._____ would send delegates there when it was

necessary to act on matters of common concern. One thing this committee did was establish the

3._____, a set of rules to loosely hold the states together. By 1786 George

4._____ and some others knew that changes were needed. They

suggested to the Congress that all the states send 5._____ to a

6._____ in Philadelphia. There they would gather to revise the old

Articles thus making the 7._____work better. When enough

8._____ had assembled, the group elected Washington as

9._____ of the convention. Because they knew that there would be many

arguments, they kept the 10._____ secret. Before each meeting, doors

were locked, 11._____ were stationed in the hall, and windows were kept

closed. Many ideas were proposed including the 12._____ by Edmund

Randolph. This plan called for three branches of government—the executive, the legislative, and the

13._____—all of which still exist today. Many points were argued over,

but probably none caused more concern than how to represent the states in

14._____. Finally, the 15._____ was

hammered out. After four long, hot months of deliberations the 16._____

was born.

Constitutional Fill-In

Use the words from The Constitutional Story on page 19 to fill in the spaces below.

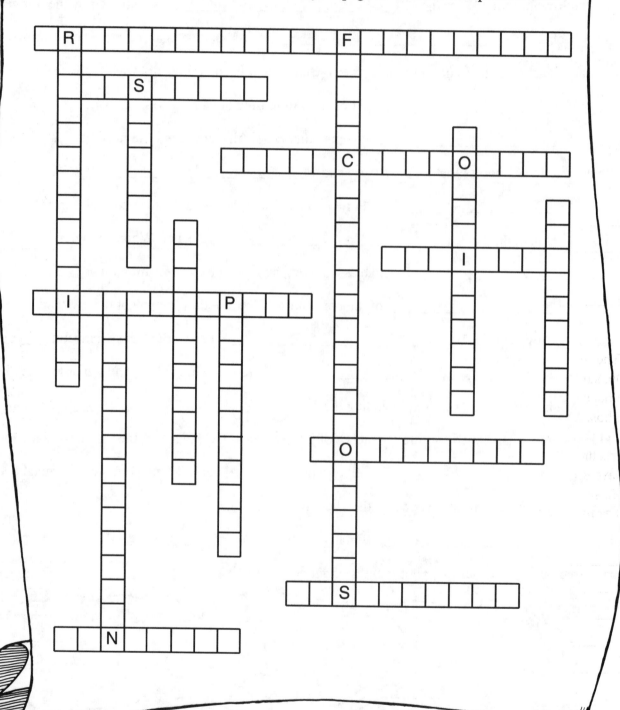

Songs of the Era

Here are the words of two songs that you probably already know. The first one, "Yankee Doodle," was written in the 1600s. British soldiers sang it to make fun of the poorly dressed colonial troops during the French and Indian War (1754-1763). It later became popular during the Revolutionary War. Music for "The Star-Spangled Banner" was originally written in the 1700s, but new words were added in 1832 by Francis Scott Key as he watched the battle rage over Fort McHenry.

Read the words to both songs. On the lines provided, write new lyrics. You may work with a partner to complete this assignment.

"Yankee Doodle"
Yankee Doodle went to town a-riding on a pony;
Stuck a feather in his cap and called it macaroni.
Yankee Doodle, keep it up, Yankee Doodle dandy,
Mind the music and the step, and with the girls be handy.

_____

_____

_____

_____

"The Star-Spangled Banner"
Oh, say, can you see, by the dawn's early light,
What so proudly we hailed at the twilight's last gleaming,
Whose broad stripes and bright stars, through the perilous fight,
O'er the ramparts we watched were so gallantly streaming?
And the rocket's red glare, the bombs bursting in air,
Gave proof through the night that our flag was still there.
Oh, say, does that Star-Spangled banner yet wave,
O'er the land of the free and the home of the brave?

_____

_____

_____

_____

_____

_____

_____

Art Activities

Celebrate the Constitutional era with any of the following art activities. Use those which are most appropriate for your students. Assign them to the whole class, small groups or pairs, or give the students a choice of the activities.

Commemorative Plates

Materials: round paper plates, old magazines, scissors, glue stick, board or cardboard (from cereal boxes, shoeboxes, etc.)

Directions:

- Instruct the students to make a commemorative plate that celebrates Constitutional times. Have them work in pairs.
- Direct them to choose a person or event from that era that they would like to depict.
- Tell them to cut out appropriate pictures and words from the magazines.
- Arrange the pictures on the paper plate and glue down.
- Make a stand or holder for the plate by cutting a 6" x 6" square of tagboard or cardboard.
- Fold the top 3" of the tagboard backwards; fold 1" of the front section upwards (see diagram).
- Rest the plate on the lip that is formed.

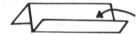

Concept Collage

Materials: tagboard or cardboard (from cereal boxes, shoeboxes, etc.), white glue or glue sticks, old magazines and newspapers, scissors

Directions:

- With the class brainstorm a list of words and phrases that describe the Constitution (supreme law of the land, a miracle, etc.).
- Divide the students into groups and assign each one a different phrase to use as a title for their collage.
- Have them cut out photos, pictures, and words that express their title.
- Display all the finished concept collages.

Silhouette Portraits

Establish that silhouettes or shadow portraits were popular in the 1700s. The word itself comes from the French Minister of Finance, Etienne de Silhouette, who made these portraits as a hobby.

Materials: white butcher paper, masking tape, opaque projector or a lamp without its shade, pencil, black construction paper, scissors, glue

Directions:

- Students will need to work in pairs on this project.
- Tape the butcher paper onto a wall.
- Move the opaque projector or the lamp about 8' from the wall.
- Place a chair sideways about one foot from the wall; have one partner sit in it.
- Adjust the projector or lamp so that the shadow is sharp.
- Have the other partner carefully trace the outline onto the paper with the pencil.
- Cut out the silhouette and glue it to a sheet of black construction paper.

22

Electrifying Experiences

Benjamin Franklin was a man of many talents. He was a statesman, writer, inventor, and a scientist among other things. One of his most memorable experiments involved a kite, a key, and a storm cloud. In order to investigate the changes in storm clouds, Franklin flew a kite into a billowing storm cloud. He had tied a key to the end of the kite line. When the electrical charge ran down the wet kite line it finally hit the key where sparks flashed. It is a wonder that Franklin was not killed or injured!

Learn about some of the properties of electricity with the following projects.

Static Electricity Chamber

In a storm cloud static electricity is formed when tiny water droplets and ice particles rub together. This results in lightning. Another kind of static electricity can occur when clothes rub together. Ask students to tell about a time when they experienced static electricity. Have the students make their own static electricity chamber.

Materials: colored art tissue, scissors, box with plastic lid (such as a stationery box)

Procedure: Supply each group with the materials listed above. Challenge them to use those materials to demonstrate static electricity in action.

Solution: Cut the tissue into squares or any small shape. Place six or eight of them into the box and cover with the lid. Rub a hand across the lid. Watch as the tissue shapes rise to the surface of the lid.

Predicting Static

Materials: paper, wood, rubber, plastic and glass objects (such as foam, paper, and plastic cups, glass jars, large craft sticks, an eraser, plastic comb); wool cloth; torn bits of tissue paper; paper and pencil

Procedure: Divide the class into pairs or small groups. Supply each group with the paper, wood, rubber, plastic, and glass objects.

- Instruct them that in turn they will rub each material with the wool cloth and then hold it above the bits of tissue to test whether the materials are attracted or not.
- Before beginning any experimentation tell the groups to determine which materials will create static electricity. Have them record their guesses on a sheet of paper.
- Direct them to circle those materials that they think will make the best static electricity.
- Have them test their hypotheses. Discuss the results in whole group.

Static Demonstration

Explain to students what you are going to demonstrate. Have them predict what will happen. Discuss the results. Afterwards, let them re-create the experiment on their own.

Materials: plastic comb, wool cloth, slowly running tap water

Procedure: Rub the comb with the cloth. Hold the charged comb next to the running water. Watch as the water moves away from the comb.

Meet Jean Fritz

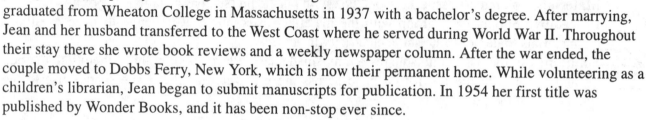

From 1987-1992 the National Education Advisory Committee to the Commission on the Bicentennial of the United States Constitution planned joint national projects to encourage American students to understand and appreciate the Constitution. It is fitting that author Jean Fritz was part of this organization since she was more than a little familiar with the topic. Her book, *Shh! We're Writing the Constitution,* had been published the same year the committee convened. Ms. Fritz's continued interest in that particular historical era led her to write another book. This one was about an important Constitutional figure, James Madison, and is titled *The Great Little Madison* (G.P. Putnam's Sons, 1989).

Jean Fritz always had an interest in writing. When she was young she wrote poetry. In college she studied English and graduated from Wheaton College in Massachusetts in 1937 with a bachelor's degree. After marrying, Jean and her husband transferred to the West Coast where he served during World War II. Throughout their stay there she wrote book reviews and a weekly newspaper column. After the war ended, the couple moved to Dobbs Ferry, New York, which is now their permanent home. While volunteering as a children's librarian, Jean began to submit manuscripts for publication. In 1954 her first title was published by Wonder Books, and it has been non-stop ever since.

To date Jean Fritz has written more than forty titles, many of which have been critically acclaimed. *Homesick: My Own Story* received five different awards, including the 1983 Newbery Honor Book and the ALA Notable Children's Book. *Shh! We're Writing the Constitution* was given the ALA award and it was named Notable Trade Book in the Field of Social Studies. In addition, for her body of work Fritz has been awarded five different honors, such as the 1986 Laura Ingalls Wilder Award and the 1985 Hans Christian Andersen Award.

When asked about her favorite project, she admits that *Homesick* (her fictional biography) is the one she feels closest to. Other books which have been fun for her to research include *Can't You Make Them Behave, King George?* and other short biographies. With *The Great Little Madison*, Fritz claims she heard James Madison himself nagging her to show that the signing of the Constitution was not the end of the story.

These days Ms. Fritz writes daily in her upstairs study following breakfast and *The New York Times*. First she revises her previous day's work. Then she writes new material in pencil before working on her IBM Selectric typewriter. No computers for this author.

Extensions:

- Find out more about the author from the series *Something About the Author* in the reference section of the library. Also, see the article, "Is that a Fact, Jean Fritz?" in the August 1984 issue of *Instructor* Magazine.
- Direct the students to write using the same style as *Shh! We're Writing the Constitution.*
- Have the students write a letter to Jean Fritz telling her what they think her next book subject should be and why.

We the People

by Peter Spier

Summary

At first glance, this book might be dismissed as a picture book that is inappropriate for use with older students. It does, however, contain much more than pictures. The introductory section gives a good background explanation of the events that led to the Grand Convention. This is followed by the Preamble presented among a collage of pictures. In the last section of the book is the complete Constitution of the United States and all of its amendments. Finally, a reproduction of the original Constitution is printed on the last two pages.

Although it is not necessary to use the text of *We the People* for this section, you will need to have copies of the Constitution available for the students. The accompanying activities and projects are written for the challenging level, and only a few are correlated to the pictures in *We the People*. Simply eliminate those if you are not using *We the People*.

Sample Plan

Lesson 1

- Prepare a Preamble bulletin board (see page 77).
- Display books about the Constitution.
- Make posters (see #3 on page 26).
- Construct a chart of rights vs privileges (see #2, page 26).

Lesson 2

- Read We the People.
- Give the Amendments Pretest on page 32.
- Review and outline the first four pages.
- Memorize the Preamble.

Lesson 3

- Rewrite the Preamble in modern language.
- Preview questions about the Constitution (#4 on page 26).

- Read the Constitution. Use the Constitution Study Guide, page 30, for outlining and paraphrasing (#5, page 27).
- Flow Chart of how laws are passed (page 37).

Lesson 4

- Read the Amendments to the Constitution.
- List ratification adtes for each amendment (page 34).
- Make a Big Book of Constitutional Amendments (page 35).
- Senate vs House Worksheet (page 36).

Lesson 4

- Mapping. Research and label a map of the 1700s (page 38).
- Math. Amazing Facts worksheet (page 39). Learn about author Peter Spier (page 40).
- Posttest. See #5 on page 27.

Overview of Activities

Setting the Stage

1. Prepare a Preamble bulletin board display. You will find a copy of the Preamble on page 28 and directions for assembling the bulletin board on page 77.

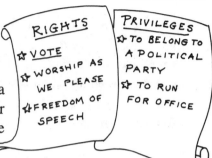

2. Discuss the differences between rights and privileges. Construct a chart that lists some of our rights as U.S. citizens and some of our privileges. Talk about how these rights are guaranteed by the Constitution and its amendments.

3. Make posters to display around the room. Label each one with a different phrase from the Preamble. For example, one poster may say, "We the People of the United States." The next one, "in Order to form a more perfect Union," etc. Display the posters for a few days. When you are ready to introduce the topic, hand out the posters to different students. Direct them to line up in correct Preamble order. Have the remaining students read the Preamble together out loud.

4. Assign students to read *We the People* by Peter Spier.

Enjoying the Book

1. **Book Reviews.** Briefly review the facts presented in the first four pages of the text of *We the People*. Divide the students into groups and have them do any of the following activities:
   - Outline the first four pages of text (which should be just a review).
   - Observe the pictures. Compare the scenes from the 1700s to those of modern times.
   - Write an appropriate text or script for the book.

2. **Learn about the Preamble.** A copy of the Preamble can be found on page 28. Introductory and extension activities follow on page 29. They include choral reading, handwriting, creative writing, vocabulary building, art, language, research, and discussion projects. Choose those which best suit your needs.

3. **Constitution Study Guide.** Make copies of page 30 for the students. Before reading each Section of the Constitution, read the corresponding information on that page. Have them add more information to each section as study of the unit studies progresses.

4. **Understanding the Constitution.** On the chalkboard or overhead projector list the ten questions on page 31. Review them with the students and tell them to look for answers to these questions as they read the text of the Constitution. Alternate methods for using that page are also provided.

Overview of Activities

Enjoying the Book (*cont.*)

5. **Paraphrasing.** After the class has read the Constitution, divide them into groups and assign the students to paraphrase what they have read. Rewrite the Constitution as a modern document. Share the finished products in whole group discussions.

6. **Study the Amendments.** Read and discuss the meaning of the Constitutional amendments. Give a copy of pages 33 and 34 to students for use as a study guide. Reinforce concepts, expand vocabulary, and develop critical thinking skills with any of the amendment activities on page 35.

7. **Knowledge Check.** Assess students' knowledge of the Senate versus the House of Representatives with the activity on page 36.

8. **From Bill to Law.** Use the flow chart on page 37 to set up a simulation of how federal laws are passed. Make the following signs: House of Representatives, Senate, House Committee, Senate Committee, Conference (or Joint) Committee, President, and a two-sided sign with Bill on one side and Law on the other. Assign students to the roles indicated on the signs and arrange the groups around the classroom. The student representing the bill should move from group to group in appropriate sequence changing the sign to the Law side when that goal is accomplished. You may wish to watch some televised sessions of Congress and its committees so that students can really get into their roles. Try several scenarios: e.g., the bill does not get out of committee, the houses do not like the compromise of the conference committee, the president vetoes a bill, etc.

Extending the Book

1. **Mapping.** Students can work in pairs to complete this mapping and research project. Have them label the map on page 38 with the information listed at the top of that page. Some research may be required to find out the correct dates and names.

2. **Amazing Facts.** Page 39 is a fun activity designed to review the math concept of squaring numbers while learning some interesting facts about the Constitutional proceedings. Assign this as an individual or group project.

3. **Create a Class Constitution.** Conduct class meetings in which a class constitution is written. After it is completed, assign groups to copy different sections onto poster board or butcher paper. Display prominently on a wall.

4. **Learn more about the author.** Share the information about author Peter Spier (see page 40) with the students. Have them research other facts about him. Find out what other books by Spier they are familiar with or have read.

5. **Posttest.** Retest the students with the amendments test from page 32. Compare the results with the pretest scores.

6. **Conduct an in-depth study of one of the founders of our Constitution.** Lesson plans for a unit on James Madison can be found on pages 41 to 60.

The Preamble

We the People of the United States,

in Order to form a more perfect Union,

establish Justice, insure domestic

Tranquility, provide for the common

defense,

promote the general Welfare,

and secure the Blessings of Liberty to

ourselves and our Posterity,

do ordain and establish this

Constitution for the

United States of America.

28

Preamble Activities

Introduce, teach, and extend the Preamble with any of the following activities. They can be employed as individual, paired, or group activities at your discretion. Choose those which best suit your classroom needs.

1. Give each student a copy of the Preamble (page 28) to study.

2. Record the Preamble. Let students listen to it to help them memorize it. Call on a few students each day to recite the Preamble in front of the class.

3. Conduct a choral reading of the Preamble. Have the whole class participate in this activity. Record their reading on audio- or video-tape. Replay it and criticize it constructively. Rerecord if necessary.

4. Copy the Preamble. Direct the students to copy the paragraph in their best handwriting. Encourage the use of real ink pens. For a fancy effect, try felt-tip calligraphy pens. If possible, invite a calligraphy expert to class to demonstrate some techniques to the students.

5. Rewrite the Preamble in modern language. Tell the students to share the new version with a partner. Create a display with the modern versions. Place a copy of the Preamble in the center of a bulletin board and attach the modern versions around the Preamble.

6. Find out what the word *Preamble* means. Find other examples of preambles in other documents (possibly in your state's constitution).

7. With the students discuss the meaning of the prefix *pre*. Instruct them to make a list of at least 25 words that begin with the prefix *pre*.

8. Make a Preamble collage. You will need a supply of old magazines and newspapers for this activity. Direct the students to cut out letters, words, and/or syllables from the magazines and newspapers. Assemble the words and glue them to a sheet of tagboard, card stock, or other heavy paper. Make a frame or draw a fancy border around the words. Display all the Preambles.

9. Supply each student group with a copy of the Preamble. Have them circle all the verbs; replace each one with a synonym. Read the new Preamble. Share them in whole group discussions.

10. Research and find out who wrote the Preamble. How was it received among the delegates?

11. Write a class preamble. As a whole group discuss purposes and goals as students attending that school. Together write a preamble expressing those purposes. Assign some students to make a large poster of the class preamble and display it proudly.

12. Discuss the importance and significance of the Preamble to the Constitution. What are some of the key words and phrases in the paragraph?

We the People

Constitution Study Guide

The following outline lists some important features contained in each of the articles of the Constitution. This page may be used as a study guide for students. Ask students to add more information to each Article as they read and learn about the Constitution.

Article I	Rules for forming and running Congress are outlined. In addition, it divides Congress into two houses, the House of Representatives and the Senate. Basic requirements for candidates for the House and the Senate are stated. Duties of each house are given. The powers of Congress are listed.
Article II	This article gives the President the power to carry out the nation's laws. It says that the President's term of office is four years. Procedures for electing the President are provided. Requirements for presidential candidates are listed. The President's powers are enumerated. Finally, it outlines grounds for the impeachment of the President.
Article III	In Article III the Supreme Court is established. It lists all cases over which the judicial branch has power. A definition of treason is stated along with a listing of laws for dealing with treasonable behavior against the United States.
Article IV	A state may not treat a citizen of another state differently from its own citizens. Congress is given the power to admit new states to the union.
Article V	The provisions for amending the Constitution are listed in this article. It requires that three-fourths of the states approve an amendment before it becomes law.
Article VI	This article makes the Constitution the supreme law of the land and says that all Federal and state officials are required to support it.
Article VII	This last section says that at least nine states will be required to ratify the 1787 Constitution, at which time it will become the law of the land.

Constitution Quiz

Check students' knowledge and understanding of the seven articles of the Constitution with the following questions. Use any of the following methods. For easy reference, sample answers have been provided at the bottom of the page.

- Discuss them a few at a time in whole group discussion.
- Write one question on the board daily. Direct the students to write answers. Pair the students and have them share their responses.
- Cut apart the questions and give one to each student pair or small group. In turn, have the groups present the question and their answer to the whole class.

1.	What are the requirements of candidates for the House of Representatives?
2.	How were representatives apportioned?
3.	What are the requirements of candidates for the Senate?
4.	How is the number of senators determined and how long is their term?
5.	How does a bill become a law?
6.	What are five powers given to Congress?
7.	What are the requirements of a candidate for the Presidency?
8.	What are three duties of the President?
9.	How does the Constitution define treason?
10.	How can the Constitution be amended?

ANSWERS

1. Must be at least 25 years of age, a citizen for 7 years, and an inhabitant of the state from which elected. 2. One for every 30,000 free men; 3 slaves would be counted for every 5 free men. 3. Must be at least 30 years of age, a citizen for 9 years, and an inhabitant of the state from which elected. 4. Two for each state; term is 6 years.

5. Either house introduces a bill; if it passes both houses, it is sent to the President. He signs it to become a law, but if he vetoes it, he sends it back to the house where it originated. After reconsideration, if two-thirds pass it the bill goes to the other house. And if two-thirds there also pass it, the bill becomes a law. 6. To collect taxes and duties, to borrow money, to regulate commerce with foreign nations, to establish rules of naturalization, to coin money, to punish counterfeiting, to establish post offices, to promote science and useful arts, to institute courts, to define and punish piracy, to declare war, to raise armies, to maintain a navy, to call up the militia. 7. Must be a natural citizen, at least 35 years old, and have resided within the U.S. 14 years. 8. Act as commander-in-chief of the army and navy, make treaties, appoint ambassadors and other public officials, provide Congress with a state of the union. 9. Levying war against the U.S., siding with and providing aid and comfort to the enemy. 10. Two-thirds of both houses must pass the bill, and then three-fourths of the states must ratify it.

Amendments Pretest

Tell the students to label sheets of paper with their names, the date, and numbers from 1 to 27. Read the following directions aloud to the students: "I am going to read a list of rights we have as citizens of the United States of America. Each of these rights is guaranteed by an amendment to the Constitution. After I have read a statement, write the number of the amendment cited." NOTE: For easy reference, answers appear at the bottom of this page. Record the results of this assessment. At the end of the unit, administer this test again and compare results.

1. Women were given the right to vote.
2. The legal rights of people in criminal cases are guaranteed, including the right to a fair trail.
3. This amendment provides that U.S. senators be elected directly by the people.
4. Powers not given to the federal government belong to the states.
5. Slavery was abolished.
6. This early amendment stated that soldiers could be lodged in private homes only with the owners' consent.
7. It repealed the eighteenth amendment.
8. Listed in the Bill of Rights, it preserves the right to trail by jury in civil cases.
9. It requires that choices for President and Vice-President be designated.
10. This gives state militias the right to bear arms.
11. Congress may impose individual federal income tax.
12. Unreasonable searches and seizures are prohibited.
13. The President is limited to serving two terms.
14. This outlines the procedure for presidential succession in case of presidential disability.
15. It protects freedom of religion, speech, press, and assembly.
16. The manufacture and sale of alcohol is prohibited.
17. The payment of a tax may not be used as a requirement to vote.
18. This amendment lowered the voting age to 18.
19. The right to vote cannot be denied because of race.
20. This amendment forbids courts to set unreasonably high bail and also forbids cruel and unusual punishment.
21. Federal courts are prohibited from hearing cases lodged against a state by a citizen of another state.
22. The President and Vice-President begin their terms on January 20 while members of Congress begin theirs on January 3.
23. Citizenship is defined; all persons born or naturalized in the United States are considered citizens.
24. Even though all rights are not listed in the Constitution, the people still retain those rights.
25. Washington, D.C., is given the right to vote for President and Vice-President.
26. This protects the rights of people in criminal cases. An accused must be told the charges against him and be allowed a lawyer.
27. Congress cannot pass an immediate salary increase for itself. Salary increases cannot take effect until after the next congressional election.

Answers: 1. XIX; 2. V; 3. XVII:,4. X; 5. XIII; 6. III; 7. XXI; 8. VII; 9. XII; 10. II; 11. XVI; 12. IV; 13. XXII; 14. XXV; 15. I; 16. XVIII; 17. XXIV; 18. XXVI; 19. XV; 20. VIII; 21. XI; 22. XX; 23. XIV; 24. IX; 25. XXIII; 26. VI; 27. XXVII

Bill of Rights Study Guide

When the Constitution was originally written in 1787, it did not contain a Bill of Rights. However, the delegates made provisions for such a future measure. In 1791, ten amendments consisting of only 462 words were added to the Constitution. On this page, you will find a study guide to the first ten amendments to the Constitution. Brief explanations after each one will help you understand the rights that are guaranteed by that amendment.

BILL OF RIGHTS

Amendment I Guarantees and protects **freedoms of religion, speech, press, assembly, and petition.**

Amendment II Gives **the people the right to bear arms** or keep weapons, since a well-regulated militia is necessary to the security of a free country.

Amendment III Says that providing **lodging for soldiers** in private homes is only permissible with the consent of the owner.

Amendment IV **Prohibits unreasonable searches and seizures**, and requires a warrant if there is probable cause or reason to believe that a search will produce evidence of a crime.

Amendment V Outlines **legal rights of people in criminal proceedings**. Before being brought to trial for a felony, **a person must be charged with a specific crime**. Persons **may not be tried twice for the same crime**. A person **cannot be forced to give testimony against himself** in court. Persons accused of a crime are entitled to due process—that is, a fair hearing or trial. The **government may not seize private property for public use without paying** the owner a fair market price.

Amendment VI Protects the **rights of people in criminal cases** and guarantees the right to a speedy and public trial. The accused must be told the charges against him and must be allowed to have a lawyer.

Amendment VII Preserves the **right of trial by jury in civil cases** or cases involving parties contesting private matters.

Amendment VIII **Forbids unreasonably high bail** to be set by courts. Also, **punishment may not be cruel or unusual** (such as torture).

Amendment IX Provides that **the people retain certain rights**, even though the Constitution does not specifically list them.

Amendment X Says that **powers not given to the federal government belong to the states**. This amendment limits the power of the federal government.

Amendments Study Guide

In the years following the passage of the U.s. constitution, twenty-seven amendments have been added to the document. The first ten, or the Bill of Rights, have already been outlined on the previous page. On this page, you will find brief explanations of each of the remaining seventeen amendments.

Amendment XI   Prohibits federal courts from hearing cases lodged against a state by a citizen of another state (ratified February 7, 1795).

Amendment XII   Requires that choices for President and Vice-President be designated as such (ratified June 15, 1804).

Amendment XIII   **Abolished slavery** (ratified December 6, 1865).

Amendment XIV   **Defined citizenship** as all persons born or naturalized in the United States (ratified July 9, 1868).

Amendment XV   Declares that the **right to vote cannot be denied because of race** (ratified February 3, 1870).

Amendment XVI   Gives Congress the power to impose individual **federal income tax** (ratified February 3, 1913).

Amendment XVII   Provides that United States **senators be elected directly** by the people (ratified April 8, 1913).

Amendment XVIII   Prohibits the manufacture, sale, and shipment of **alcoholic beverages** (ratified January 16, 1919).

Amendment XIX   Gives **women the right to vote** (ratified August 18, 1920).

Amendment XX   States that the **President and Vice-President** begin their new terms on **January 20**; members of **Congress** begin on **January 3** (ratified January 23, 1933).

Amendment XXI   **Repealed the 18th amendment** (ratified December 5, 1933).

Amendment XXII   Limits the **President** to serving **two terms** (ratified February 27, 1951).

Amendment XXIII   **Washington, D.C.,** is given the **right to vote** for President and Vice-President (ratified March 29, 1961).

Amendment XXIV   **Prohibits** the payment of a **tax as a requirement to vote** (ratified January 23, 1964).

Amendment XXV   Outlines the procedure for **presidential succession** in case of presidential disability (ratified February 10, 1967).

Amendment XXVI   Lowers the **voting age to 18** (ratified July 1, 1971).

Amendment XXVII   **Congress cannot pass immediate salary increases** for itself (ratified May 7, 1992).

Follow-Up Amendment Activities

Reinforce concepts, expand vocabulary, and encourage critical thinking skills with any of the following activities.

- Make a Big Book of Constitutional Amendments. Divide the students into small groups and assign them a number of amendments. Direct them to write in Roman numerals the number of the amendment at the top of a sheet of paper. In modern language, rewrite the amendment. When all groups have completed their writing, arrange the pages in chronological order on the wall in a column (or see #4 on page 77, Bulletin Boards).

- Look at the ratification dates listed for amendments XI through XXVII on page 34. Direct student pairs to make a chart showing when each of these amendments was proposed and when they were finally passed. Find out which law took the longest to be ratified and which took the least amount of time.

- Divide the students into pairs and instruct them to write a new amendment that they would actually like to see added to the Constitution. Have the pairs exchange their bills with another pair. Discuss any changes they think should be made in the wording and return the bills to the other pair. Have them discuss whether or not they think such a measure could really be passed by Congress. In whole group discuss each pair's ideas.

- Write Congressional representatives. Have the students find out the names and address of their representatives in Congress. As individuals, pairs, or small groups, students can write a letter to a Congressperson concerning a matter of importance (possibly about their rights as citizens). Address envelopes to the Congresspeople and mail at your discretion. Another option is to assign groups to trade letters with one another and answer the letter as they think that Congressperson might.

- Recreate a mock Congress. Divide the class into two groups, the senators and the representatives. Direct the representatives to initiate a bill. After they have composed a proposal and a majority votes to pass it, they should send it to the senators by messenger. (Students may choose a speaker to do this.) The senate debates and changes the proposal, if necessary, and after a majority accepts it, presents it to the president (the teacher or a chosen student). If the bill is vetoed, it goes back to the representatives where two-thirds must vote for passage. Next it goes to the senate and again, two-thirds must vote for the bill before it can become law. Follow up with the flow chart on page 37.

- Make a giant class chart of the first ten amendments and the rights guaranteed by each one. Use butcher paper and colored markers. Have the students highlight important words in the explanation of each amendment and draw a picture of each one in action.

- Assign students to read other books or articles that contain information about the Constitution and the amendments. NOTE: Some excellent sources include *The Bill of Rights* by Milton Meltzer, *This Constitution* by Peter Sgroi, and *Cobblestone*. (See the Bibliography on page 79 for specific issues.) Tell them to research in-depth some current issues such as gun control, capital punishment, taxes, etc., and find out in which sections of the Constitution these ideas are discussed. Follow these topics in the news and share any stories that might pertain to these subjects.

Senate vs. House

Perhaps the fiercest arguments during the Congressional Convention came when the delegates began to determine how power should be divided in the government. States with large populations wanted to be represented in Congress by population count, but the less-populated states thought this arrangement was unfair. Eventually a compromise was reached. It was called the Great Compromise, and it established some rules for Congress that both sides were able to agree upon.

Read the statements below. As a group, determine if each statement is true of the Senate only, the House of Representatives only, or if it is true for both. Circle the *S* if the sentence is true for the Senate only; circle *H* if the statement is true for the House only; circle both the *S* and the *H* if the statement is true for both the Senate and House members.

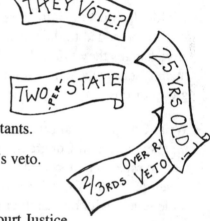

1. S   H   Each state has only two members in it.

2. S   H   To qualify, a person must be a citizen for seven years.

3. S   H   They vote on bills.

4. S   H   A candidate must be at least 25 years old.

5. S   H   It would allow one representative for every 40,000 inhabitants.

6. S   H   Two-thirds of them are required to override the President's veto.

7. S   H   Members serve a term of six years.

8. S   H   They must approve the President's choice for Supreme Court Justice.

9. S   H   A person must be a citizen for nine years to qualify to become one.

10. S   H   They are members of Congress.

11. S   H   They serve a term of two years.

12. S   H   This has the most members.

13. S   H   Bills can start here.

14. S   H   Its candidates must be at least thirty years old.

15. S   H   They choose a Speaker as their leader.

16. S   H   Its President is the Vice-President of the United States.

17. S   H   They have the sole power to hold a trial for all impeachments.

18. S   H   Members must be an inhabitant of the state in which they are chosen.

Challenge: On the back of this paper make a Venn diagram using all the statements listed above.

How Laws Are Passed

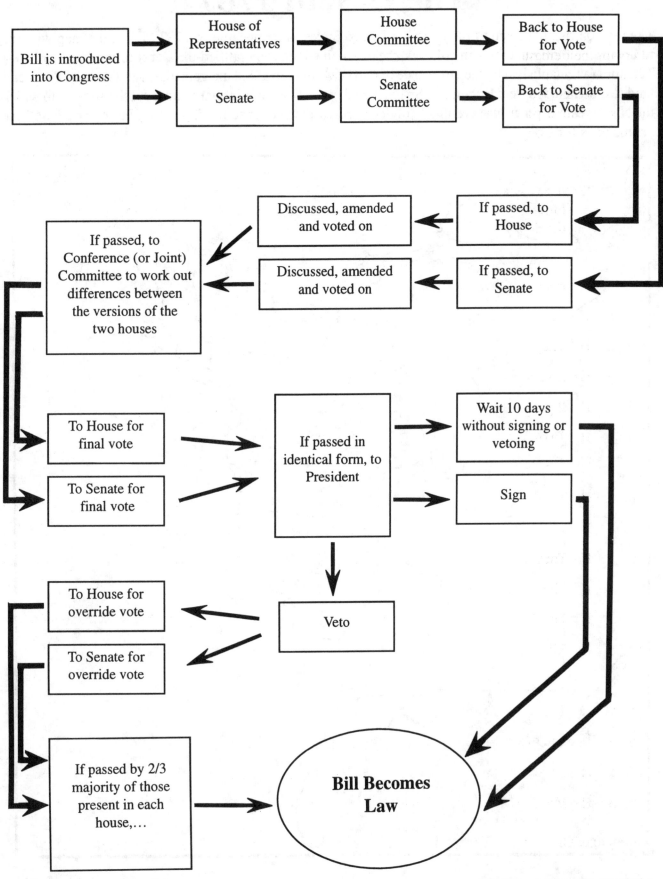

The U.S. in 1787

The map on this page shows the fledgling United States as it appeared in 1787. Label the map with the following: the original thirteen colonies, the dates on which each ratified the Constitution, the Northwest Territory (as established by the Ordinance of 1787), undivided U.S. land gained by the Treaty of Paris, and land still owned by Great Britain and Spain. Challenge: Draw border lines and label the states into which the Northwest Territory was eventually divided. Show the date of admission to the Union of each of these states.

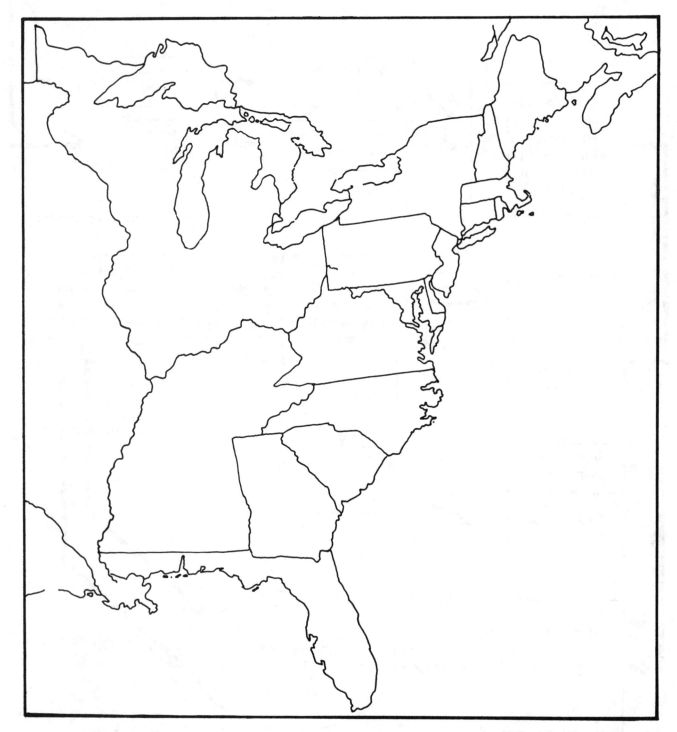

Amazing Facts

Complete the problems on the left. Write each answer on the line provided within each sentence. Read the sentence to find an amazing fact about the Constitutional times.

1. 1,000 squared

    The population of the United States at this time was under _____ people.

2. 5 squared + 1

    The youngest delegate was Jonathan Dayton of New Jersey; he was _____ years old.

3. 10 squared

    In some places tea cost more than _____ dollars a pound.

4. sq. root of 36

    Among the delegates, _____ had signed the Declaration of Independence.

5. sq. root of 25

    _____ of the delegates to the Convention had signed the Articles of Confederation.

6. 4 squared + 3

    _____ delegates never showed up for the Convention for personal reasons and lack of support of the idea.

7. 20 squared + 10 squared

    After the Constitution was inscribed on parchment, the Convention ordered _____ copies of it to be printed.

8. 50 squared - 563

    The name of the gifted scribe of the embellished Constitution was forgotten until _____.

9. 12 squared + 17

    James Madison gave _____ speeches, second only to Gouverneur Morris.

10. 9 squared + 4

    _____ newspaper articles written about the Constitutional events later became known as *The Federalist Papers*.

11. sq. root of 4

    When George Washington arrived at the Convention, he was escorted by three generals, two colonels, and _____ majors.

12. 7 squared - 6

    The average age of the fifty-five delegates was a little over _____.

13. sq. root of 81

    Of the delegates 26 were college graduates; _____ were foreign born.

14. 6 squared - 21

    Virginia governor, Edmund Randolph, submitted the Virginia Plan – a _____-point plan – to the delegates.

Challenge: In problem #8, who was the scribe and why was his name not remembered until 1937?

Meet Peter Spier

Artist and author, Peter Spier, was born June 6, 1927, in Amsterdam, Netherlands. He recalls his growing-up years in Broeck-in-Waterland with vivid memories. (Broeck-in-Waterland is the birthplace of Hans Brinker, hero of the novel by Mary Mapes Dodges. Ironically, not many people living in this small village have ever heard of Hans Brinker.) His brother, sister and he would walk to the tram which took them to their school in Amsterdam. In the winter they would skate to the station. The train was filled with the many smells of villagers smoking pipes and cigars and fishermen carrying baskets of herring and smoked eel to the market.

Spier's father was a famous journalistic artist and political cartoonist. Books were an integral part of their daily life and because of his father's profession they kept current on public events and politics. Sculpting people, horses, and entire towns from clay and plasticine was also an important activity in Spier's life. After deciding on a career in art, he enrolled in the Royal Academy of Art in Amsterdam where he took classes in drawing, etching, and graphics. Following art school he joined the Navy and served for three and a half years. Still, he yearned to write. In 1949 he began working for *Elsevier's Weekblad* in Paris, France. The next year he was transferred to Houston, Texas. Later, he moved to New York to work as a freelance writer. Spier became an American citizen in 1959 and now resides on Long Island in New York. He is married with two grown children.

Over the years Peter Spier has written and illustrated more than forty books and won numerous awards. *Noah's Ark* won the prestigious Caldecott Medal in 1978. Other honors include the Christopher Award, Caldecott Honor Book (for *The Fox Went Out on a Chilly Night*), American Book Award, and the American Library Association Notable Book (*Oh, Were They Ever Happy!* and *Rain*).

Activities

- *We the People* is Peter Spier's illustrated version of the Preamble to the Constitution. Instruct the students to observe the first two pages of pictures and tell them to be prepared to discuss the types of work today versus how the chores were performed in 1787. Also talk about some of the professions today that did not exist in the 1700s.
- Discuss the layout of Spier's pictorials. Establish that they are part cartoon, yet tell a story. Have the students choose one article of the Constitution to illustrate, using the same format and style that Spier employed in *We the People*.
- In his spare time Peter Spier likes to build model ships. Encourage students to bring in model ships that they have built. If possible, supply the students with some models and let each group work together to build one.

The Great Little Madison

by Jean Fritz

Summary

As a boy James Madison was pale and sickly; his voice was weak and he suffered from a form of epilepsy caused by nerves. It is hard to imagine that a child with such a fragile start in life would some day become one of the most influential men in the history of the United States of America. Accompanying his brother, William, to Princeton in 1774 was a turning point in James Madison's life. It was on this journey that he was filled with the energy of the bustling city of Philadelphia and became enthusiastic about life again. The earlier death of his schoolmate, Joe Ross, had affected him deeply, and he was obsessed with the notion that he, too, would die at an early age. That trip was just what he needed to revive his spirits and get on with his life. Later in the year he bought some property so that he could vote and hold office. When James and his father were elected to the Orange County Committee of Safety, his political career had begun. It would span years and wars and political turmoil, and it would culminate with his two terms as President of the United States of America. Author Jean Fritz writes an interesting, enjoyable account of one man's road to the Presidency. Her thorough research is apparent with the many intriguing details included throughout the text. Prints and engravings add to the spirit of the book, transporting the reader back to the late eighteenth and early nineteenth centuries. Students and adults alike will long remember the story of our fourth President.

Sample Plan

Lesson 1

- Create a class web about James Madison (page 42).
- Display a 1770s map of U.S. and discuss.
- Read an excerpt from *The Great Little Madison*.

Lesson 2

- Assign Chapters 1 to 3 for reading.
- Begin Chapter by Chapter activities (pages 44-47).
- Daily writing. See page 49 for topics.
- Vocabulary. Make flash cards (#1, page 48).
- Write About It. Assign a topic from page 54.

Lesson 3

- Assign Chapters 4 to 6 for reading.
- Continue Chapter by Chapter activities (pages 44-47).
- Continue daily writing (page 49).
- A Coded Message, worksheet on page 55.
- Comprehension. See Descriptions, #1 on page 51.

Lesson 4

- Assign Chapters 7 to 9 for reading.
- Continue Chapter by Chapter activities (pages 44-47).
- Continue daily writing (page 49).
- Fill-Ins. See #3 on page 48.
- Math. Find numbers in the text (page 56).

Lesson 5

- Assign Chapters 10 to 11 and notes for reading.
- Continue Chapter by Chapter activities (pages 44-47).
- Continue daily writing (page 49).

Lesson 6

- Causes and Effects (page 53).
- Comprehension Check (pages 49 - 50).
- Culminating Activity. Build mini museums (page 58).

Overview of Activities

Setting the Stage

1. **Create a Web**. Ask students what they know about James Madison. Record all responses on chart paper; add to it throughout the unit.

2. **Using a Map.** Display a map of the United States in the 1770s. Identify the thirteen states and territories. Compare it with a map of the U.S. in the 1830s. Briefly discuss which states had been added at that time and what the Louisiana Purchase was all about. Establish that James Madison was born in 1751 and died in 1836, living to see all these changes.

3. **Define Biography.** On a piece of scrap paper have the students write the elements that make for a good biography. Share the writings in whole group discussion. Call on some students to tell about their favorite biography and why they liked it.

4. **An Introduction.** Read the first paragraph aloud to the students. Have them infer what kind of a President James might be. Record the responses on chart paper or the overhead projector. Save for later use.

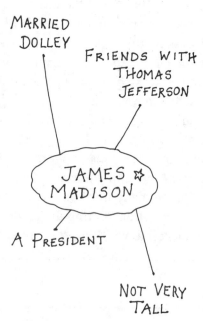

Enjoying the Book

1. **Reading.** Assign a number of chapters for reading each day. Suggested amounts are specified in the Sample Plan on page 41.

2. **Chapter by Chapter**. Reinforce each chapter's reading with the corresponding activities on pages 44 through 47. Assign students to complete all the listed activities for each chapter or give them a choice of which ones to work on.

3. **Vocabulary Activities.** Suggested vocabulary words for each chapter can be found on pages 44 - 47. Add or delete words as necessary. Incorporate these words into your curriculum with any of the activities and projects found on page 48.

4. **Comprehension Check.** Assess students' comprehension with some of the questions on pages 49 to 50. These questions may be used as daily writing topics, story prompts, class discussions, written assessment tools, or even for review. Sample answers are provided for easy reference.

5. **Comprehension Strategies.** Different methods for developing comprehension are outlined on page 51. Modeling and brainstorming are suggested means for preparing students for an assignment, especially when they may need a review or an introduction to the concept. Choose those ideas which best suit your style of teaching and classroom needs.

Overview of Activities *(cont.)*

Enjoying the Book *(cont.)*

6. **Comparing.** Madison and Jefferson were friends and political allies for many years. On page 52 students can make a chart that shows just what good friends these men really were. Have students add five more items of their own to the chart.

7. **Cause and Effect.** Page 53 contains an overview of the critical thinking skill termed cause and effect. Also included on that page are a number of causes and effects taken straight from the pages of *The Great Little Madison.* It can be used as an oral exercise or as a written assignment.

8. **Creative Writing.** Twelve different story prompts are provided on page 54. Assign them to students as outlined on the page or write two or three topics on the board. Allow students to choose one. Although the directions on page 54 tell you to time the students' writing, it is not necessary to do so.

9. **A Coded Message.** Madison and Jefferson developed a code that they used in their frequent correspondence. Students can sample this code with the worksheet on page 55. Challenge the students to work with a partner and devise a code of their own. Have them share it with another pair.

10. **Math.** On page 56 you will learn how easy it is to develop math problems based on this literature selection. Sample word problems and lessons based on *The Great Little Madison* are also provided.

Extending the Book

1. **Washington vs. Madison.** In this activity on page 57, students will not only write summary statements but they will also compare two great leaders. Complete how-to's are provided at the top of the page.

2. **Mini Museums.** This is a great way for students to culminate a unit of Constitutional studies and to show what they have learned and accomplished during the time period. Divide the students into groups for this synthesis project on page 58. Directions are given for preparing appliance boxes. Suggested artifacts to make and acquire are also listed. Share the finished products with other classes or invite family members to attend a viewing.

3. **Constitutional Players.** On pages 59 and 60 you will find picture biographies of eight men who played a role in the formation of the Constitution. Learning activities for these cards can be found on page 58. Extend the idea by having students make biography cards for Alexander Hamilton, Aaron Burr, John Adams, Thomas Jefferson, Patrick Henry, Dolley Madison, Lafayette, Captain Oliver Perry, and other characters in the James Madison biography.

4. **Reports.** Assign individual students to write reports on topics of their choice. Some guidelines can be found on pages 66 to 68.

Chapter by Chapter

As students read the chapters, assign any of the following activities to assess comprehension and knowledge, encourage research skills, and develop vocabulary. At the beginning of each chapter's activities you will find a list of suggested vocabulary words. (Add or delete from the list as necessary. Ways to expand vocabulary can be found on page 48.) This list is followed by a number of projects, some of which are complete with corresponding worksheets or lessons.

Chapter I

Vocabulary: plantation, shriveled, froth, bilious, seizures, epilepsy, diagnosed, logic, devoured, inevitable, obsessed

- Draw a map of Virginia and the three other states (Maryland, Pennsylvania, and New Jersey) through which Madison traveled from his home in Virginia to Princeton University.
- James' father called him "Jemmy." Write a creative story telling how you think he got his nickname.
- By age eleven James had read all 85 of his father's books. How many books have you read in your lifetime? List them (or as many as you can remember).

Chapter II

Vocabulary: exercise, toleration, inconspicuous, tyranny, eloquent, quartered, imbecilic, sentiments, revision, adjourned, breeches, opponent, devoutly, perishing, ascertained

- "Women spent entire afternoons dressing their hair into such towering beehives that when they went out in the evening, they had to scrunch down in their carriages to keep their hairdos from scraping the roofs." Draw a picture of this scenario.
- In a letter to Jefferson, Madison said, "Congress needed more power; it needed better statesmen; it needed permanent solutions, not flimsy patchwork measures; and it certainly needed money." From Madison's point of view, write that letter to Jefferson stating your concerns.
- Madison and Jefferson had developed their own code to ensure secrecy. With a partner create your own code and message. Trade your message with another pair and see if the words can be deciphered. (For a coded message worksheet see page 55.)
- Compare Madison and Jefferson. Draw a chart or Venn diagram which shows their likenesses and differences. (See page 52 for a prepared lesson.)

Chapter III

Vocabulary: balked, makeshift, monarchy, commercial, petition, insurrection, chaos, sovereignty, resolution, contradiction, supreme, unpredictable, scurried, diligent, reverberate, harrowing, inalienable, retained, intent, indentured servant, revolt

- During the Constitutional proceedings the issue of slavery was hotly debated. Madison said that prolonging the slave trade was "dishonorable to the American character." Explain this statement.
- Sometimes in the evenings Madison would play a game of whist with his family. Whist was a card game that was a forerunner of bridge as we know it today. Find out how to play bridge. Describe the deck of cards needed to play and list some of the rules. For a real challenge learn how to play bridge.

Chapter by Chapter *(cont.)*

Chapter III (cont.)
- Pretend you are a news reporter for the *Federal Times*. Word of Shay's Rebellion has just reached your office. Go out on assignment and interview Daniel Shay. Work with a partner and choose roles as Shay or the reporter. Write an interview of questions and answers concerning the uprising. Rehearse the script before presenting it to the class.

Chapter IV
Vocabulary: proponents, infuriated, diplomatic, monumental, blunder, harangue, whit, spellbinder, tranquility, transfixed, shackled, conviction, confederated, indispensable, inaugurated, unbridled, rivulets, helm

- Construct a time lime of dates and events of when the new government would officially take over. (See page 53 of *The Great Little Madison* for dates and events to include.)
- On page 54 there is a vivid description of George Washington's inauguration. After reading that page, draw a picture of one of the events.
- If possible, find a copy of *The Federalist Papers* and read one or more of the essays.

Chapter V
Vocabulary: skeptical, infringed, Susquehanna, confrontation, certificates, incentive, virtuous, secede, aristocracy, oppressed, drastic, gadgets, redeem, speculators, public securities, sheaf, manipulate, crucial, mutual, persistent, collaborated, accusations, republic, isolation, alliance

- Find the Susquehanna and Potomac Rivers on a map. What states do the rivers run through? How far is the Susquehanna from the present capital of Washington, D.C.?
- From France, Jefferson sent Madison some of the latest gadgets available in that country. They included phosphorescent matches, a pocket compass with a spring stop, a portable magnifying glass that fit into a cane, and a pedometer. Research and find out some other inventions in the late 1700s.
- Explain what Hamilton and Madison each proposed to do about the debt problem. What compromise was finally reached?

Chapter VI
Vocabulary: epidemic, contagion, informant, intimidated, restrictions, dictates, eluding, lenient, hostility, envoy, effigy, staunch, querulous, pompous, contempt, ominous, tactic, maneuvers, nullify, peerless.

- What is yellow fever? Find out about its symptoms, causes, and cures. Is it prevalent today? Why or why not?
- Describe the events that led to the Whisky Rebellion. How did Hamilton react to the uprising?
- Explain the provisions of the Alien Act and the Sedition Act. Why did Jefferson write the "Kentucky Resolves" and Madison the "Virginia Resolves"?

Chapter by Chapter *(cont.)*

Chapter VII

Vocabulary: diverted, folderol, pell-mell, cupola, ally, vassal, code, orator, pretense, intolerable, revelled, inconsolable, rabid, despicable, indicted, compunctions, inevitable, confiscating, blockade, impressed, soliciting, conspirator, arbitrary

- Draw a map of the United States as it looked in 1803. Label the Louisiana Purchase Territory, the Spanish Territory, the Oregon Country, and the thirteen states.
- Dolley Madison loved to shop, and she became famous for her high fashion. She was especially fond of wearing turbans on her head and dresses with an Empire style. Make a list of ten other First Ladies and write about their contributions to fashion.
- Look at the political cartoon on page 102. Draw a political cartoon that shows public sentiment regarding the Embargo Act of 1807.

Chapter VIII

Vocabulary: confection, levees, propensity, deplored, frivolous, premature, impertinence, calculated, decree, stucco, bas relief, inundated, dogged, conscientious

- After James Madison was inaugurated, his wife Dolley held weekly receptions where she served a delicious frozen dessert called ice cream that Thomas Jefferson had introduced from France. Make homemade ice cream using either an electric or hand-cranked ice-cream maker.
- Make a three-dimensional model of a room that Dolley Madison might have remodeled. Use a shoe box for the diorama. Keep in mind that yellow was her favorite color, she used red velvet for drapes, and she hung a life-sized portrait of George Washington in one room. (Read page 107 for more details.)
- Explain this statement: "America began its war one day after war may no longer have been necessary..." Rewrite history and tell how things might have been different if the news about England repealing their orders had reached America sooner.

Chapter IX

Vocabulary: disposed, intact, bluster, intermediary, reprimand, scoffed, blunder, aplomb

- Explain the differences in fighting styles between the British and the Americans. Which way was more effective?
- Find a copy of "The Star-Spangled Banner." In your best handwriting copy it onto a sheet of paper. As a whole class sing our national anthem. Find out how and when it became our nation's official song.
- John Armstrong was Madison's Secretary of War. Give four reasons why Armstrong proved himself to be a poor leader.

Chapter X

Vocabulary: tyrant, prolong, inducement, contended, woebegone, dysentery, rampart, simultaneous, volleys, torrential, careened, superlatives, ample

Chapter by Chapter *(cont.)*

Chapter X (cont.)
- Jackson had only half as many troops as General Packenham, yet Jackson was easily able to defeat the British at the Battle of New Orleans. Explain why the Americans had the advantage.
- The steamboat was newly invented in 1817 when Madison took office for his second term. Draw and label the parts of a steam engine and explain how one works.
- What was the Treaty of Ghent and when was it signed? How might things have been different if mail service had been as fast as it is today or if faxes and telephones had been available?

Chapter XI
Vocabulary: feebler, exuberant, ebullient, coincidences, pessimist, industrialized, nullification, precedent, defiance, tedious, cherish, perpetuated, obelisk, subscription

- Describe the Madisons' daily routine at their retirement home in Montpelier. Tell what hobbies each enjoyed.
- In 1829 Andrew Jackson succeeded Monroe as President of the United States. By this time there were 23 states. List them.
- Make a list of the first six U.S. Presidents and their Vice-Presidents. Write the dates of their administrations.

After-the-Book Activities
- The chapters in this book are untitled. After reading one, write an appropriate title for that chapter. Share your title and the reason for it with a partner.
- As a class, brainstorm all the contributions that James Madison made for our country's government. Vote on the top five most important ones.
- With a partner or in a small group, list some of the difficulties Madison faced as President. Discuss how he handled each one and tell whether you think he was effective. How do you think he could have done better in some situations?
- In whole group discuss Madison's strengths and weaknesses. Construct a chart showing examples of each.
- Write a creative story about the friendship between Madison and Thomas Jefferson. Include how they helped and supported each other throughout the years.
- Make up a list of events in Madison's own personal life like his schooling at age eleven, the death of his best friend, etc. Make a time line of these events. Assign a different one to each pair of students. Direct them to write the event on a large index card and draw a picture to illustrate it. When all the cards are completed, arrange them in correct chronological order and attach them to a clothesline. The index cards can also be displayed across the chalkboard tray.
- Tell how life changed in the years James Madison was alive (1751 - 1836). What new products were invented? How did fashions change? How did the United States grow?
- Compare a map of the United States in 1787 to one of the U.S. in 1836. What changes had taken place? What was the population in 1836 versus 1787?

Vocabulary Activities

On this page you will find a number of interesting and unique ways to introduce, reinforce, and expand vocabulary words. Use the suggested word lists on pages 44 to 47 or create your own. Employ those techniques that best suit your purposes.

1. **Flash Cards I.** Make a line down the center of a sheet of unlined paper. Draw two-inch strips across the same page and write a different vocabulary word in each space. Make as many copies of the pages as you will need. Students can cut out the rectangles and write a definition of the word on the back of the paper. Use as a paired activity and have students quiz one another on the spellings or the definitions of words.

2. **Flash Cards II.** Mount flash cards with tagboard or other heavy paper. Display the cards on the chalkboard tray. Highlight a number of words each day, defining them and using them in sentences. Encourage the students to use these words in their conversations at home that evening. The next morning discuss which words they were able to use.

3. **Fill-Ins.** Display a copy of the vocabulary words on the chalkboard or overhead projector. You should also have individual student copies available. Prepare a number of sentences from the text and delete one word from each. Ask students to reread the sentence and supply the missing word. For example, "When the _____ was over, Dolley and little Payne returned to Philadelphia at about the same time as James Madison returned." (Correct response: epidemic)

4. **Fill-Ins Extension.** Assign a number of words to each student pair or group. Direct them to find examples of their vocabulary list in the literature selection and prepare sentences with one missing word. Have them take turns presenting their fill-in sentences to the rest of the class.

5. **Progressive Assignment.** Divide the students into groups of three. Give the first person in each group a set of index cards (one for each vocabulary word) and tell them to copy a different vocabulary word on each card. Underneath the vocabulary word write a definition. When each person is ready, have him or her pass the cards on to the next member who writes each word in a sentence. The third member divides each word into syllables and tells its part of speech.

6. **Obsolete Words.** Many words that may have been popular years ago are seldom heard today (e.g., woebegone, folderol, levees). Direct student groups to scan the text of the literature selection to find obscure or obsolete words. Make a class chart of the words and their meanings.

7. **Choices.** Give students a number of assignments to choose from. For example, you may write five projects on the board and give students one week to complete any three of them. Some suggestions: write a creative story using any ten of the vocabulary words; alphabetize all the words and divide them into syllables; find each word in the text and copy the whole sentence in which it appears; write all the dictionary definitions of each word; write a homonym, synonym, or antonym for each word.

48

Questions, Questions

Use the questions on this page for comprehension checks, story prompts, class discussions, or daily writing activities. Sample responses appear after each question.

- How would you describe the young James Madison? (small, pale, sickly boy with a weak voice; subject to liver upsets, fever, and seizures)
- How did James react to his friend Joe Ross' death? (became depressed and obsessed with the idea of dying young)
- Did the journey to Princeton with his brother William help or hurt James? (It helped because he became excited with the city's activity; he bought 2 acres of his father's farm so he could vote and hold office.)
- Why did he lose his bid for the Virginia House of Delegates? (His opponent treated voters to whisky at the polls.)
- Why did Madison call the Articles of Confederation "imbecilic"? (because the states were only interested in maintaining their own rights and Congress had no power to force the states to do anything for the central government)
- How would you characterize the Marquis de Lafayette? (the French general active in the American revolution; an open, friendly, enthusiastic figure who was popular with the American people)
- How did Shay's Rebellion contribute to interest in the Philadelphia convention? (Congress had no money or militia to stop the insurrection.)
- What were Madison's views concerning slavery? (hated it; thought it was "dishonorable to the American character" to continue the practice)
- What is the importance of *The Federalist Papers*? (They described to the public how the Constitution was going to work.)
- For what two reasons did Madison support a Bill of Rights? (to keep a promise; saw that it would actually help the courts)
- What did Hamilton propose to do about the debt problem? (to sell government bonds at 6%, to redeem old certificates for full value, to assume all the states' debts)
- What did Madison propose to do about the dept problem? (sell land in the Western territories, consider tariffs on whiskey and higher taxes on countries which did not have and agreement with the U.S.)
- What were the main differences between the Republicans' beliefs and the Federalists'? (Republicans were friends of the Union, put faith in the people, and were against public debt; Federalists did not trust people to govern themselves.)
- Why did Great Britain go to war in 1789 against France during that country's revolution? (They were alarmed at the way French extremists were trying to spread their revolution to other countries. They thought they would be next, so they made the first move.)
- How did people try to cope with the yellow fever epidemic? (burned tar, sprinkled clothes with vinegar, people walked in the middle of the street)
- What was the Whisky Rebellion? (A small group of farmers were protesting a whisky tax; after petitions went unheeded, they began tarring and feathering those who opposed them.)
- How did Great Britain make it difficult for the U.S. to remain neutral in the war with France? (Royal Navy seized food or ships bound for France, captured ships in the West Indian ports, stopped American ships at sea, and sometimes took American sailors.)

Questions, Questions *(cont.)*

- What were the terms of the 1798 Alien Act? (allowed the President to deport aliens who were citizens of an enemy nation in case of war or threat of war)
- What was the Sedition Act? (forbade writing or speaking against the government or President with the purpose of bringing them into contempt)
- What did Jefferson and Madison do in response to the Sedition Act and Alien Act? (Jefferson wrote the "Kentucky Resolves" and Madison wrote the "Virginia Resolves" protesting that the two acts were unconstitutional.)
- How did "the Pope of Rome on the Tiber" get his nickname? (Landowner Francis Pope called his property Rome and the stream next to it was called the Tiber.)
- Why did Aaron Burr challenge Alexander Hamilton to a duel? (felt Hamilton was responsible for his defeat in the race for governor)
- What was the Embargo Act and why was it passed? (No more trade would be allowed with Europe. It passed because England and France were confiscating U.S. ships and goods.)
- What made Dolley Madison so popular? (reintroduced inaugural balls; held weekly receptions; was very fashionable; redecorated mansion)
- What was the Hornet's mission? (to bring word to the British that 25,000 U.S. men were being enlisted and all duty and merchant vessels were being armed)
- What event made Captain Oliver Perry famous? (captured an entire British squadron on Lake Erie)
- What are some reasons you think Secretary of War John Armstrong was a poor leader? (lied to Madison, answered mail on his own, gave orders without the President's permission, did not believe British would attack Washington)
- Which state papers did Madison order removed to the safety of Virginia? (Declaration of Independence, the Constitution, President Washington's letters)
- What did the British do when they reached the capital? (sat in House of Representatives and voted unanimously to burn the city down)
- Where had Payne been during this time? (in Paris, France, gambling and leading a wild life)
- Why was Andrew Jackson called "Old Hickory"? (because he was so tough)
- What advantages did the Americans have over the British in the Battle of New Orleans? (were able to duck behind ramparts to reload, fired all the time; British fired in systematic volleys and had to march forward without being able to reload)
- What was the Treaty of Ghent? (peace treaty with Britain signed December 24, 1815, fifteen days before Battle of New Orleans)
- What was "the house with a thousand candles?" (Seven Buildings, the temporary home of the President and his wife, so named for its 31 windows which Dolley kept illuminated)
- What money problems did Madison have in his retirement? (had not been able to save any of his salary; Payne was constantly in debt)
- What coincidence occurred on the fiftieth anniversary of the Declaration of Independence? (Both John Adams and Thomas Jefferson died.)
- What did John C. Calhoun's doctrine of nullification state? (that if a state did not like a federal law it did not have to obey it; if the federal government tried to force that state to obey, it had the right to secede from the Union)
- What happened to Dolley after Madison died? (She had to sell Montpelier and move to Washington, D.C., where she was welcomed like a returning queen.)

Developing Comprehension

Help students develop, expand, and use the critical thinking skill of comprehension with any of the ideas presented on this page. Model a particular idea with the whole class if they are unfamiliar with the process involved. This will help them to understand exactly what is expected of them. Also, it is a good practice to begin each skill lesson with a quick brainstorming session to help students get started. Student pairs or groups may do their own brainstorming, or you may want to conduct a whole class session.

1. **Descriptions.** Describe something a character did in the story action. Explain why he or she did it. (For example, Madison finished school in two years. Why? Possibly because he was following the example of his best friend who had less money for many years of school.)

2. **Changes.** Choose one character from the story. Tell what changes he went through from the beginning of the story until the end. (Madison was shy and barely spoke in public. His experiences in public office gave him the confidence to become outspoken.)

3. **Sequencing.** Work with a partner. On separate sheets of paper, both partners should write five different events that occurred in the story. Exchange papers and rewrite the events in correct chronological sequence. Discuss your answers with your partner.

4. **Background**. Discuss with the students some of the clues found in *The Great Little Madison* that told them about the setting of the story (maps, pictures, text, dates, etc.).

5. **Comparing**. As a class, draw comparisons between two of the characters in the story. Comparing Madison and Washington would be one example. Make a chart or a Venn diagram to show their likenesses and differences. (Both were important historical figures and served as U.S. President; Washington was a great war hero; Madison was sickly and could not serve in the military; etc.) For a prepared lesson on a comparison between these two men, see page 57.

6. **Comparing II.** In another comparison activity, direct the students to compare two stories (in this case, two biographies). For example, after they have read *The Great Little Madison* and a biography of Washington or Jefferson, discuss what elements the two books have in common (setting, plot, characters, actions, ending). Talk about ways the two are different (author's style, language used, development of characters, etc.).

7. **Listing.** With the class, discuss some of the main character's accomplishments; record the responses on the chalkboard, overhead projector, or chart paper. Instruct the students to fold a sheet of drawing paper in half and then in half again. In each segment list one accomplishment and draw a picture to illustrate the event. Use both sides of the paper.

8. **Purpose.** Ask students to discuss why they think a particular author wrote a book. Have them give an explanation as to why they feel this way. (Why Jean Fritz wrote *The Great Little Madison*: she thinks he was a great man who deserved more recognition for what he did as a politician and President. This is evident from the way she describes him, events, and the consequences of his actions.)

Madison and Jefferson

The lifelong friendship between James Madison and Thomas Jefferson began when Jefferson was elected to succeed Patrick Henry as governor of the state of Virginia. Madison discovered not only how well he and Jefferson worked together, but also how much they had in common. Read through the listings below. Determine which things they both liked and which they both did not like. Write each phrase in the proper section of the chart on this page.

slavery	experimenting with science	talking about history
a vision of a strong united republic	reading	Great Britain
planting trees	collecting books	Patrick Henry
the lopsided Virginia constitution	serving their country	public speaking
newfangled gadgets	entering into a war	corresponding

Both Liked	Both Did Not Like

Challenge: Add at least five more facts to this chart. You may have to do some research to complete this activity.

Causes and Effects

Cause and effect is an important critical thinking skill that can easily be taught through the use of a literature selection. This page shows one way this can be done.

Cause and Effect

Establish that in the cause-and-effect relationship, a **cause** is the reason something happens and the **effect** is the action that takes place in response to the cause. Read this example: "When James Madison heard that his schoolfriend Joe Ross had died, he became depressed and feared that he would also die young." The cause in this case is Joe Ross' death. The effect is that Madison became depressed and fearful that he, too, would die young.

Listed below are some causes and effects to discuss with the students. Present the causes and let them come up with the effects. When they are comfortable with the process, supply them with an effect and ask them to name the cause. This lesson can be conducted orally or as a written assignment.

CAUSE	EFFECT
Madison accompanied brother William to Princeton.	He bought two acres of land so he could vote and hold office.
Connecticut, New Jersey, and Delaware had declared themselves duty-free ports.	This destroyed trade in states where duties were enforced.
Great Britain was alarmed at the way French extremists tried to spread the revolution.	Great Britain went to war against France.
Madison realized he couldn't win the battle of the debt problem.	He compromised with Hamilton.
France was angry with Jay's treaty and the election of John Adams.	France ordered the American minister out of their country.
The Tiber was diverted.	It became Pennsylvania Avenue.
Aaron Burr blamed his defeat for governor on Alexander Hamilton.	He challenged Hamilton to a duel, which he won.
The *Leopard* followed the *Chesapeake* out of its port and demanded to search it.	Jefferson declared American waters off-limits to Britain.
Jefferson wanted to protect the U.S. from possible interference from France.	He purchased the Louisiana Territory.
In 1807 the Embargo Act was passed.	No more trade was allowed with Europe.
Americans aimed at the waterline of ships.	They were able to sink them.
Madison began getting his notes in order.	He wanted them to be printed after his death.

Write About It

Reproduce this page as many times as you need to and cut out the creative writing topics on the dark lines. Place the cut-apart topics into a shoe box or other container and let students draw one. Have pairs of students brainstorm ideas for their stories. Set a timer for twenty minutes and direct the students to write on their chosen topic for that time period.

It is the year 1824. General Lafayette is coming to your hometown to visit. Tell what preparations your family and town will make for his tour.

You think your best friend would make the perfect wife for the unmarried James Madison. In an introductory letter to your friend, describe Madison and tell her all about his accomplishments.

As Daniel Shay, write a speech convincing your fellow farmers why they must march to the federal arsenal in Springfield, Massachusetts, and what they must do when they get there.

As the wife of an important delegate, you have been invited to the mansion for one of Dolley Madison's famous parties. Describe the food and events.

Your newspaper has been given the scoop about the Hamilton-Burr duel. As a witness to the event, write a news feature describing the duel.

Madison hated the idea of slavery, yet he knew it would be too costly to run a plantation without the help of slaves. What are some alternatives Madison might have explored?

Alexander Hamilton spoke for six hours on why he thought the President of the U.S. should serve a life term. What are some of the things you think Hamilton might have said during that six-hour speech?

At the time of Madison's presidential term, there were two political parties, the Republicans and the Federalists. Which one would you have chosen if you were alive then? Explain why.

In order to protect the U.S. from possible commercial interference by France, Thomas Jefferson bought the Louisiana Territory. How might the U.S. be different if this purchase had not been made?

Captain Oliver Perry captured an entire British squadron on Lake Erie. As Captain Perry, explain to President Madison some of the tactics you used to help win the battle.

President Madison and his wife Dolley knew that the British were going to attack Washington, D.C. Dolley began to pack things for safekeeping. If you were Dolley, what would you have saved?

American lawyer Francis Scott Key witnessed Fort McHenry's victory over the British and even wrote a song about it called "The Star-Spangled Banner." Write a poem describing the events. (Keep in mind the words of the song.)

54

A Coded Message

James Madison and Thomas Jefferson corresponded faithfully throughout the years of their friendship and they even developed a code for their personal use. Meant to insure secrecy, this complicated code consisted of pages of words arranged alphabetically. Each word was then followed by a number which was used to replace words in the letters they wrote to one another.

See if you can write the correct message using the code words below.

about 84	criticized 38	Madison 101	restrictions 17
agreement 137	Embargo Act ...152	obvious 27	same...............30
all 19	England 61	off 49	the 80
an 72	failure 99	office 64	to 28
and 107	furious 37	over 32	trade...............60
both 15	in 20	policy 48	unpopular.........78
but 106	incident...........62	ready 88	was 56
called 70	Jefferson 103	reminded 100	were 26
Chesapeake 45	King George 77	repeal 24	while 95

_____ _____ _____ _____ _____
15   103   107   101   26

_____ _____ _____ _____ _____
38   32   80   30   48

_____ _____ _____ . _____ 1807 _____
95   20   64   80   152

_____ _____ _____ _____ _____ _____. _____
56   78   107   72   27   99   61

_____ _____ _____ _____ _____ _____
56   88   28   24   19   60

_____ _____ 1809 _____ _____ _____
17   20   106   101   100

_____ _____ _____ _____ _____
77   84   80   45   62

_____, _____ _____ _____ _____ _____.
37   77   70   49   80   137

Math From the Pages

Are you searching for ways to incorporate math lessons into your literature or thematic-based program? The answer can often be found right on the pages of the literature selection which you are studying. This page will tell you what to look for in the text which can help incorporate math into your lesson. Sample activities for *The Great Little Madison* follow these directions.

Looking for Math

- When previewing the text, look for numbers and numerals. Examples: James Madison grew up on a 5,000 acre farm; he was 5 feet 6 inches tall; by the age of eleven he had read all 85 of his father's books.
- Determine which skills you want to introduce, teach, and reinforce. Develop an activity based on that skill and the numbers which you have found. For example, if you are reviewing the conversion of feet and inches, you could ask students to determine how many inches tall Madison was.
- Think of some word problems that can be created with information found in the text. Example: James and his friend, Joe Ross, finished their last two years of college in one year. At that rate how long would it take them to complete 8 more years of college? (Answer: 4; divide 8 by 2.)
- Assign students to look for examples of numbers in the text. As a whole group, brainstorm possible math activities, lessons, or word problems.

Math from *The Great Little Madison*

- Convert Madison's height from feet and inches to meters and centimeters. Convert the number of acres of the farm (5,000) to square feet, square yards, or square miles.
- On a map, measure the distance from James' home in Montpelier, to Princeton, New Jersey, where he attended college.
- The Federalist Papers consisted of a total of 85 essays. Alexander Hamilton wrote 51; James Madison wrote 29; and John Jay wrote 5. Write a fraction for each. Figure out what percentage of the papers each man wrote.
- Only nine states out of thirteen were needed to ratify the Constitution before it became the law of the land. Write a fraction to show this and then find a percentage. If eleven signatures had been required, what percentage of all the states would this be?
- Have students read a specific chapter of the book and tell them to jot down every example of a number that they find. In small groups discuss different ways numbers are used, such as measurement, dates, ages, etc. Direct them to fold a sheet of lined paper in half lengthwise. In one column, they will list all the numbers they found. In the second column on the corresponding line, they should then write the numbers in words (e.g., five thousand rather than 5000).
- Massachusetts ratified the Constitution by a margin of 187 to 168. How many members of the legislature were there altogether?
- Dolley Madison had three large mirrors installed in the Capitol at a total cost of $2150. If each mirror cost the same amount, what was the price of each mirror?
- General Packenham had 10,000 troops in his command. Andrew Jackson had only half as many. How many troops did Jackson have?
- As President, Madison had been unable to save any of his $25,000.00 salary. How much money was that per year? (Hint: He served two terms.)

Washington vs. Madison

Both George Washington and James Madison were key figures in the Constitutional Convention. Although the two came from different backgrounds and each had his own distinct personality, they both agreed that the thirteen states needed a strong central government.

Use the following activity to assess students' knowledge of these two leaders and as a means to provide practice in writing skills, particularly summarizing.

- Direct the students to fold a sheet of lined paper in half to form two columns.
- Have them label the paper with their name and the correct date.
- At the top of the left column, have them write *Washington*; at the top of the right column they should write *Madison*.
- Tell the students that you are going to write a number of statements on the chalkboard (or use the overhead projector). Some statements will tell about Washington while others will refer to Madison.
- After carefully reading a sentence, they should paraphrase or summarize it in note form in the proper column on their folded sheet.
- Give students an example. Write this sentence on the board: "He was the one person whom all people and all parties trusted." Ask how this statement might be summarized. One possible response: "trusted by all people and parties." Ask where this note belongs (in the Washington column).

Listed below are a number of statements which can be used for this activity. For easy reference, answers are provided below. If a transparency is made of these statements, be sure to cover up the answers.

1. He was a very large man for his time and the way he carried himself made him seem even larger.
2. The greatest of all war heroes in America, he led the French and Indian War and the Revolution.
3. In Virginia and in Congress, he had a reputation as a bright young man who wrote well.
4. His brief education was received at home.
5. At the Convention he was considered the mind of America.
6. He dressed in black and led a very quiet social life.
7. A short man, he was also very slim and boyish and had a soft voice.
8. Everyone addressed him as general, even his wife.
9. For his time he was well educated; he graduated from Princeton University.
10. He was a very social man and was always the center of attention at parties.
11. Some call him the heart behind the new nation as he did the daily work which was needed.
12. Because he was sickly most of his life, he was not able to fight in the Revolution.

Answers: 1. Washington; 2. Washington; 3. Madison; 4. Washington; 5. Madison; 6. Madison; 7. Madison; 8. Washington; 9. Madison; 10. Washington; 11. Washington; 12. Madison

Culminating Ideas

Wrap up your Constitutional studies with either of these two projects. Some prepared pages to help you get started are included in the second activity.

Mini Museums

In this culminating activity, student groups will create their own mini museums complete with artifacts. Divide the students into large groups. Each group will need a large appliance box (like one from a refrigerator) and the following directions.

- Paint the inside walls of the box with white paint, allowing plenty of time for the paint to dry.
- Each group may work in private behind their own box. Close up the boxes at the end of the day until the museums are ready to be opened.
- Each group will be responsible for making artifacts from the era such as quills, hornbooks, a copy of the Preamble on parchment, etc. (For directions for these projects see page 8.) Attach the artifacts to the inside walls.
- Research periodicals, particularly *Cobblestone*, a history magazine for young students. (For specific issues see the Bibliography on page 79 of this book.) Write reports about people and events of the times to include in the museum.
- Read the daily newspaper to find articles that may have a connection to the Constitution. Display these articles on the museum walls.
- Brainstorm with the class to think of anything else that might be appropriate for the museums.
- After the museums are completed, share them with other classes, the principal, and family members. Provide a tour on a specified day.

Constitutional Players

Pictures and biographies of eight different delegates to the Constitutional Convention can be found on pages 59 and 60. Here are some ways to use them, but there are many possibilities.

- After copying the pages, mount them on tagboard, index stock (available in copy stores), or other heavy paper. Cut the biographies out, laminate, and store in a labeled manila envelope. Student pairs can quiz each other using the cards. For example, one partner draws a card from the envelope and reads a sentence from the biography. The other partner must guess the delegate. If necessary, another clue can be read. Assign students to make new cards for other delegates which can be added to the cards in the envelope.

- Make two copies of the Constitutional Players cards, blocking out the text on one set and blocking out the pictures on the other set. Mount both sets on tagboard. Cut out, laminate, and store both sets in a labeled manila envelope. Write playing directions on the front of the envelope. One possibility is a concentration game where they match the picture with the biography.

- Use pages 59 and 60 to create a mini book. Make copies of both pages for each student. Cut apart the biographies and assemble into a book. Assign students to add more biographies of their own.

58

The Constitutional Players

George Washington

Born: 1732
Died: 1799
Birthplace: Virginia
Delegate from Virginia

Important Facts: He was unanimously elected as president of the Constitutional Convention. Previously, he had been a delegate to the Continental Congress of 1774-1775. During the Revolutionary War of 1775, he was appointed as Commander-in-Chief of the Continental Army. It was largely at his urging that a strong united government was instituted. He served as the first President of the United States.

Benjamin Franklin

Born: 1706
Died: 1790
Birthplace: Massachusetts
Delegate from Pennsylvania

Important Facts: The oldest of the delegates, he was in such ill health that he had to be carried to the meetings. This multi-talented man wrote *Poor Richard's Almanack*; was a newspaper publisher; built the first free library in the colonies; invented the lightning conductor, Franklin stove, and bifocals; and served as a diplomat to foreign nations. He also helped with the drafting of the Declaration of Independence.

James Madison

Born: 1751
Died: 1836
Birthplace: Virginia
Delegate from Virginia

Important Facts: Although he was slight in stature, he was long on knowledge. He proposed many of the ideas adopted by the Constitutional Convention and he kept careful notes of the proceedings. He is called the Father of the Constitution. Previously, he had served as a member of the Continental Congress. With the support of long-time friend Thomas Jefferson, he was elected President in 1809 and served two terms.

Edmund Randolph

Born: 1753
Died: 1813
Birthplace: Virginia
Delegate from Virginia

Important Facts: A member of a well-known Virginia family, he went on to serve as that state's governor from 1786-1788. At the Grand Convention he proposed the Virginia Plan whose ideas formed the basis of the Constitution. Despite his participation at the convention, he did not sign the Constitution. However, he did later ratify it. In 1789, he became the first U.S. Attorney General and its first Secretary of State (1794-1795).

#582 Thematic Unit—U.S. Constitution

The Constitutional Players *(cont.)*

Elbridge Gerry

Born: 1744
Died: 1814
Birthplace: Massachusetts
Delegate from Massachusetts

Important Facts: People sometimes called him "Grumbletonian" behind his back. His motion that the plan for a constitution begin with a bill of rights was unanimously defeated. Consequently, he was among the few who refused to sign the document. He is remembered as a defender of states' rights and personal liberty. He went on to serve as a Vice-President under James Madison.

Alexander Hamilton

Born: 1755
Died: 1804
Birthplace: West Indies
Delegate from New York

Important Facts: At the Convention, he supported the document as written and argued that a bill of rights was unnecessary. A powerful statesman, he co-authored *The Federalist Papers* with John Jay and James Madison. He served as the first Secretary of the Treasury and became leader of the Federalist Party. During John Adams' presidency, he was killed in a duel with his political opponent, Aaron Burr.

Gouverneur Morris

Born: 1752
Died: 1813
Birthplace: New York
Delegate from Pennsylvania

Important Facts: Known as "The Tall Boy" of the convention, he lobbied for a strong federal government. He also served as a literary adviser and was responsible for much of the wording of the Constitution. From 1792-1794, he served as a minister to France. He also played a large part in promoting the Erie Canal. In addition, he is credited with planning the U.S. decimal coin system.

Roger Sherman

Born: 1721
Died: 1793
Birthplace: Massachusetts
Delegate from Connecticut

Important Facts: With Oliver Ellsworth's help, the Connecticut Compromise was introduced. This plan called for both proportional and equal representation in Congress. After some slight changes on Benjamin Franklin's part, the proposal was finally accepted. From 1789 to 1791, he served as a U.S. representative and from 1791 to 1793, he was a senator for the state of Connecticut.

The Constitutional Times

Writing a class newspaper is an excellent culminating activity for this unit. Students will be able to exhibit their knowledge of the era as well as the events and people that they have learned about. In the process, they will be employing creative writing skills and working cooperatively in groups to achieve a common goal. On these four pages you will find a suggested outline of types of stories to include in the newspaper. (For more information on writing class newspapers see Teacher Created Materials #137, *Newspaper Reporters.* Prepared newspaper outlines are also available from Teacher Created Materials - #138, *Newspapers.*) NOTE: In writing this newspaper, remind students to think like the people who took part in the formation of the Constitution and to be particularly aware of the time period itself.

1. **The Staff.** Every newspaper has a staff of team members with specific tasks to perform. Usually there is an editor in charge of coordinating all departments. A news department provides feature stories and illustrations for the pages of the newspaper. In the business department, the staff prepares classified ads. Finally, the layout department determines the order of the pages and how the articles and features will appear on the pages. Act as editor yourself or appoint a student to the job. Together, choose heads for each department and assign students to each group. Make a chart that shows the chain of command. For a prepared sheet see page 63. You may want to add a proofing department which checks all articles for grammar, punctuation, spelling, and language.

2. **The News Department.** Under the direction of the editor, people in the news department write and illustrate the features found in the pages of the newspaper. Some areas to be covered are listed below. In parentheses after each description you will find examples of what might have appeared in the newspaper during the writing of the Constitution. (Guidelines for writing news stories can be found on page 64.)

   - **News.** This includes writing headline stories and articles for the front page. "Madison Declares War"; "Lafayette to Visit Washington, D.C."; "Washington Unanimously Elected President")

   - **Editorial.** An editorial is a written opinion about the news, not just the facts. Sometimes editorials are accompanied by cartoons. ("Madison Calls the Articles of Confederation Imbecilic"; "Why the Federalist Party Is Right" by Alexander Hamilton; "Why the Constitution Needs a Bill of Rights" by James Madison)

   - **Features.** Here you will find any number of topics such as interviews with a certain key person; articles about travel, cooking, new products; etc. ("Traveling with Lafayette" by James Madison; "Dolley Madison's Secret Recipe for Ice Cream"; "An Interview with the Inventor of the Steamboat")

   - **Entertainment.** Because television, videos, movies, and anything else requiring electricity were not around yet, people held parties for entertainment. There were also plays, operas, some libraries, and games of whist. Research other forms of entertainment available then and write a story based on your findings.

The Constitutional Times *(cont.)*

2. **The News Department** *(cont.)*
   - **Art.** Since photography had not yet been invented, all cartoons and illustrations were drawn by hand. Include plenty of illustrations throughout your paper (portraits of Dolley, James, etc.; maps; newly invented gadgets).

3. **The Business Department.** The purpose of the business department is to raise revenues for the newspaper. This is done by selling newspapers, newspaper subscriptions, advertising, and classified ads. After the class newspaper has been published, you may want to sell copies of it to other classes in the school. If possible, look at manuscripts of old newspapers and discuss how papers are different today. Have the students in this department write an ad for a compass, phosphorescent matches, or any other new invention of the day. Tell them to set prices for each, keeping in mind the cost of items in the late 1700s. Others in this department can compose help wanted ads for typical jobs. Some research may be required to complete work in this area.

4. **Layout Department.** In this department the students will typeset the articles (if available use a typewriter or computer) and determine where and how all the stories will fit onto the pages. Look at a number of newspapers to observe the different styles of formatting before beginning the actual layout process. Also find examples of each of the features outlined below.
   Some features that should be included on the front page follow:
   - Masthead (the name of the paper, the date, and the city)
   - Logo (the paper's trademark may be a slogan or artwork)
   - Headlines (introductory words to an article)
   - Banner (main headline on the front page, tells about main story)
   - Subhead (found beneath a headline, it explains more about a story)
   - By-line (gives credit to the author of an article)
   - Dateline (gives the location of the story)
   - Caption (words accompanying a picture or illustration)
   - Index (a listing of all the contents of the newspaper)

   The layout can be done any number of ways including:
   a. Use a computer with a special software program.
   b. Paste up by hand. After students write a story, cut it out and place it on typing paper (if it is going to be reproduced) or sheets of tagboard. When all stories and artwork have been arranged, glue them down with rubber cement or use a glue stick.
   c. Use a typewriter. Divide a sheet of typing paper with outlines for articles. Have the students type their stories in the spaces.

5. **Proofing Department.** The staff on this department is in charge of corrections. Some things to look for include misspellings, incorrect grammar usage, use of capital letters, accuracy of facts, correct use of punctuation marks. This should be an on-going process and completed before any layout is begun. (See page 64 for a proofing chart.)

Chain of Command

Fill in the spaces with the names of the students assigned to each area. Add more spaces and departments as necessary.

Editor

News Department

Business Department

Layout Department

Proofing Department

Other

Helpful Hints

On this page are two sections which can be copied separately and used as guidelines for the students. The first section explains the important elements of story writing. The second section is a chart of commonly used proofing marks. (For more help on proofing marks see Teacher Created Materials #501, *Write All About It.*)

Writing New Stories

Every reporter knows that a good news story contains the 5 W's and How. For a great story every time, ask yourself these questions and include information about each question in your completed article. An example is given in parentheses.

WHO	is the story about? (Thomas Jefferson)
WHAT	happened in the story? (blockaded the British)
WHEN	did the event take place? (in 1807)
WHERE	did it take place? (Washington, D.C.)
WHY	did it happen? (British were threatening U.S. ships.)
HOW	did it happen? (by decree of Congress)

Challenge: You will need a partner and a newspaper for this project. Read one or more articles and find the 5 W's and How. Circle and label each of those six elements.

Proofreading Marks

Proofing and editing is the last stage before rewriting an article. To make their work more authentic and fun, introduce the students to these proofreading marks. Make a copy of the chart for each student.

≡	capitalize the letter	memorize the preamble.
/	make the letter lower case	A President serves four years.
sp.	word is misspelled	It is unconstitootional.
⊙	add a period	Read two chapters for homework
ℓ	remove a word	Madison was was a sickly boy.
∧	add a word	Who wrote Bill of Rights?
⌄	add a comma	She took papers pictures and books.
⌄	add an apostrophe	Turbans were Dolleys favorite.
∿	reverse words or letters	Payne lived in Paris.
#	make a space	The EmbargoAct was unpopular.
⌒	close the space	Every one thought he was spoiled.
¶	begin a new paragraph	full tilt. In its own way the

Challenge: Tell students to write an article containing examples of each of the errors listed in the chart. Have them trade papers with a partner and proof each other's work using the correct proofing marks. Students should then return the proofed papers to their owners and correct the mistakes on their own papers.

Constitution Word Banks

This resource page is a handy reference for various writing activities such as reports, creative writing, poetry, and social studies lessons. In addition, these terms can be used for spelling words and vocabulary development.

People to Know

George Washington	Alexander Hamilton	James Madison
Patrick Henry	Aaron Burr	Benjamin Franklin
Edmund Randolph	John Dickinson	Oliver Ellsworth
Luther Martin	Noah Webster	Gouverneur Morris
William Paterson	Roger Sherman	Jonathan Dayton
George Mason	Elbridge Gerry	Marquis de Lafayette

Groups

legislators	delegates
electors	Federalists
Nationalists	ambassadors
Congress	representatives
convention	First Continental Congress
Republicans	

Important Documents

"Supreme Law of the Land"
Constitution
Bill of Rights
Preamble
Great Compromise
Articles of Confederation
Declaration of Independence
Virginia Plan

Government Terms

federation	document
delegates	convention
constitution	federal
executive	legislative
judicial	Congress
monarchy	patriot
representative	legislature
aristocratic	electors
amendment	ambassador
ratification	

Related Items

Revolutionary War
Treaty of Paris
import duties
Shay's Rebellion
Magna Carta
Liberty Hall
New Jersey Plan
debates
Connecticut Compromise
quorum
Committee of Detail
parchment
Committee of Style and Arrangement
Treaty of Ghent

Legalese

civil rights	due process
ex post facto law	grand jury
precedent	writ of habeas corpus
double jeopardy	bill of attainder
inalienable rights	

Tips for Report Writing

Do you panic whenever the teacher assigns you to write a report? You can now relax because help is on the way. The easy hints on this page will show you how to organize your work into small, manageable steps. Follow the steps in the order listed to write a good report every time.

1. Find out everything you need to know about the assignment. What topics can you choose from? What should be included in the report (cover, introduction, bibliography, etc.)? How many pages should it contain? Should you provide maps, illustrations, or other visuals? When is it due?

2. You must choose your topic. Can't think of one? Ask a partner to brainstorm possible subjects with you or enlist the help of a parent, the librarian, or teacher. (Some Constitution-related topics can be found on page 68.)

3. Formulate some questions you may have about the subject you have chosen. Doing this will help you determine where to go to find the information you will need. At this point, put all of your questions in writing and get teacher approval before doing any actual research. (Ask your teacher about the Student Research Outline for you to use in recording your plan.)

4. Research the topic and answer the questions you have formulated in the previous step. Jot notes onto index cards. Be sure to label each index card with the resource (book, magazine, tape, etc.) in which you have found the information. Later, these can be incorporated into the bibliography of your report.

5. Arrange the questions you previously formulated in good, logical order. Using the notes from your research, write your report starting with information from your first question.

6. Proofread your first draft. Look for misspelled words, sentence fragments, capitalization mistakes, and other grammatical errors. Trade papers with a partner to see if all the sentences make sense. Possibly discuss how you can make the writing better.

7. Once you have corrected all mistakes, copy your report neatly. Even if you are using a typewriter or a computer, check your final copy one last time before turning it in to the teacher.

Use this checklist to help organize your report.

JOB	DUE DATE	COMPLETED
1. Learn about the assignment.	_____	_____
2. Choose a topic.	_____	_____
3. Formulate questions.	_____	_____
4. Research and take notes.	_____	_____
5. Write first draft.	_____	_____
6. Revise first draft.	_____	_____
7. Recopy and turn in.	_____	_____

Student Research Outline

Writing a report can seem like a difficult task unless it is broken down into manageable steps. Use this outline to help you organize and prepare your research. Read page 66 for practical tips on report writing. Some suggested topics can be seen on page 68.

1. My research topic is _____

   _____

   _____

2. The reason I am interested in this topic is _____

   _____

   _____

3. Five questions I have about this topic are:

   1. _____

   2. _____

   3. _____

   4. _____

   5. _____

4. I have checked all the resources I will use to gather information.

   Textbooks   Encyclopedias
   Literature   Information Almanacs
   Magazines   Computer Software Programs
   Newspapers   Databases
   Audio Tapes   Videotapes
   Other_____

5. I will have completed my research by _____.
                                          (date)

   Student's Signature_____

   Parent's Signature _____

   Teacher's Signature_____

Report Topics

The first step in writing a report is to decide on a topic you are interested in. Listed below are a number of suitable topics from which to choose. If necessary, a topic may be modified in order to better suit your interests.

- James Madison's role in the writing of the Constitution
- Federalist views vs. anti-Federalist views
- reasons why the Grand Convention was initially suggested
- the importance of the Bill of Rights
- how Shay's Rebellion helped the call for a strong national government
- highlights of the Virginia Plan
- Rhode Island's reluctance to participate in the Grand Convention
- Alexander Hamilton and his contributions to the Convention
- the influence of the Magna Carta on state governments
- the strengths of the Constitution
- basic platforms of the Great Compromise
- political aftermath of the Revolutionary War
- significance of the Declaration of Independence
- the drawbacks of the Articles of Confederation
- compromises the North made with the South
- the miracle of the Constitution
- the three branches of government and their separate functions
- inventors of the era and their inventions
- some important historical documents related to the Constitution
- Patrick Henry's views about the Grand Convention
- everyday life after the Revolutionary War
- important world events happening in the year 1790
- Gouverneur Morris' contributions to the Grand Convention

- how the system of checks and balances works
- daily life in Constitutional times
- the Bill of Rights and what they guarantee
- children's roles, chores, and recreations in the late 1700s
- time line of events leading to the formation of the Constitution
- scientific discoveries during this era
- the importance of Article V in the Constitution
- comparison of Madison and Washington (or any other two figures)
- schooling in the late 1700s
- War of 1812 battles fought on Lake Erie
- Captain Oliver Perry's contributions to the War of 1812
- Lafayette's friendship with Madison
- the relationship and friendship between Madison and Jefferson
- why the Louisiana Purchase was a good one
- Madison's views on slavery
- contributions of Washington, Jefferson, or Madison to the fledgling U.S.
- the feud between Aaron Burr and Alexander Hamilton
- how "Precious Payne" caused problems for his mother and stepfather
- Dolley Madison's contributions to the U.S. as First Lady
- in-depth study of one of the amendments
- why the Constitution only lists certain rights
- how persons can become naturalized citizens

Constitutional Figures

With the following lessons, students will learn many interesting facts and will review basic math skills at the same time. Presentation methods are suggested, but you may need to modify them for your particular classroom needs.

City	Population
New York	22,000
Philadelphia	34,000
Charleston	12,000
Boston	15,000

1. Copy the chart at the right onto the chalkboard or overhead projector for all to see. Ask the questions that follow and direct students to write their answers on a piece of scrap paper. Call on students to share their answers and offer an explanation of the process used. (In some cases answers have been provided in the parentheses after the problem.)
   - What is the difference in population between the most populated and the least populated cities? (34,000 - 12,000 = 22,000)
   - What is the average population of all four cities? (20,750)
   - What is the total population of the two least populated cities? (27,000)
   - How many more residents does the second most populated city have than the least populated city? (10,000)

2. When the first census was taken by the United States in the 1790s, the population figures were 3,172,000 Caucasians and 700,000 African Americans. Share this fact orally with the students and direct them to write the figures on a sheet of scrap paper. Call on students to write the number names in numerals onto the chalkboard. Once the correct numbers have been established, ask students to answer the following questions (or write out the questions on the board).
   - What was the total population of the U.S. at that time? (3,872,000)
   - Using the total U.S. population, what was the average population of the 13 states? (297,846)
   - What fraction of the population were African Americans? Reduce the fraction to its lowest terms. (175/968)
   - What percentage of the population were African Americans? (approximately 18%)

3. Establish that in the late 1700s a voyage from Boston, Massachusetts, to London, England, took approximately two months. Discuss with the whole class what additional information they would need in order to determine the average number of miles traveled per day during a typical voyage. Divide the students into groups to find a solution. Make sure each group has access to its own map or globe. When all groups have arrived at an answer, review the methods used and the solutions found.

4. Group the students and supply each group with a map of the United States in 1787. (Peter Spier's book *We the People* contains an excellent example.) Using the map's legend, have students find the number of miles the delegates from the remaining twelve states traveled from their capital cities to the meeting in Philadelphia. Direct them to make a graph of their findings. Have students find the average distance traveled from all the capitals.

Science in the 1700s

Much progress was made in the field of science during the 1700s. The first steam engine was invented which led the way for new types of water and ground transportation. Bifocals were invented, hot air balloons carried passengers, and the planet Uranus was discovered. In addition, a vaccine for smallpox was developed, saving thousands of lives. The mercury thermometer and the Celsius scale were both invented, and the modern system for naming plants and animals was instituted.

Some suggested methods for presenting these topics are discussed below. You may want to pair or group the students for these lessons or let each student choose his or her own topic.

1. **Steam Engines.** Draw and label the parts of a steam locomotive. Create a flow chart that explains how a steam engine works. (For prepared worksheets see Teacher Created Material's #295 Thematic Unit - *Transcontinental Railroad*, pages 27 and 28.)

2. **Bifocals.** Bring a pair of bifocals to class. (Thrift shops sometimes have inexpensive glasses.) Allow students to take turns wearing them and then write a story about the experience. Learn the difference between convex and concave lenses. Assign students to draw an example of each type of lens, explain how it works, and name some practical applications of each (eyeglasses, telescopes, etc.).

3. **Hot Air Balloons.** If possible, plan a field trip to a hot air balloon facility. The instructor can explain the principles of flight and may even demonstrate the balloon's engine. Challenge students to design an experiment which demonstrates how heat rises. Have them explain how rising heat is employed in launching a balloon and keeping it afloat.

4. **Uranus.** Instruct the students to draw a chart which shows the planets and their relation in size. They should include at least one interesting fact about each. Visit a planetarium. (Check local community colleges, universities, art museums, libraries, etc.) Look through telescopes to find the planet Uranus.

5. **Smallpox.** Ask students to give a report on smallpox and its symptoms, causes, and effects. Have them explain why it is not prevalent in this country today. Discuss how Edward Jenner's work may have contributed to Jonas Salk's discovery of a polio vaccine.

6. **Thermometers.** Direct the students to draw and label a Fahrenheit thermometer and a Celsius scale. Compare the boiling and freezing points of each. Learn how to convert from Celsius to Fahrenheit by using the equation F = nine-fifths C + 32. (Add 32 to the Celsius reading, multiply it by 9 and divide that by 5.)

7. **Carolus Linnaeus.** Find out about Carolus Linneas. Tell who he was, where he was from, and why he used Latin names. Direct students to make a chart of some common plants and/or animals and their scientific names.

• Read about other scientific discoveries of the era like the lightning conductor, Antoine Lavoisier's table of chemical elements, Galvani's demonstration of animal electricity, and invention of the seismograph.

In the Know

This brief study guide lists, defines, and explains six documents that played an important role in the history of the Constitution. After you have studied, test your knowledge with a partner. One partner reads the name of each document aloud, while the other partner describes the term in as much detail as possible. Then trade roles. You can also play a matching or concentration game after cutting the cards apart.

Document	Explanation
Declaration of Independence	One of the most famous documents in the world, it officially declared the American colonies free and independent from British rule. It was signed into effect on July 4, 1776.
Articles of Confederation	During the Revolution, the thirteen states wrote a set of governing rules. This document unified them in their fight against the British. Each state had only one vote and the rules could not be changed unless every state agreed.
Virginia Plan	This document did away with the "one state - one vote" rule and suggested two houses of Congress. Edmund Randolph's plan further called for three branches of government—the Executive, the Legislative, and the Judicial.
Great Compromise	An alternate plan of electing officials was designed by a specially appointed committee. In this plan, Congress would have two houses. One house (Representatives) would be based on population and in the other house (Senate) each state was considered equal with two votes each.
Constitution	This is the basic set of laws for our nation. It contains rules for writing and passing the laws which affect every citizen. A group of 55 delegates wrote these provisions during a four-month period in 1787.
Bill of Rights	These first ten amendments to the Constitution list those things that the government cannot take away from its citizens. They protect the individual from the power of the government.

Elsewhere in the World

While delegates from thirteen states gathered in Philadelphia to revise the old Articles of Confederation, important events were taking shape in other parts of the world. Have the students research some of these events. Cut apart the events found below and place them in a bag. Allow one student from each group or pair to draw one. Direct the students to write a one-page report about the event. Before beginning any research, brainstorm some resources they may want to use such as textbooks, biographies, almanacs, or periodicals. (**Note:** Not all the events cited here occurred in the year 1787, but all did take place between 1787 and 1797.)

- In 1792 Denmark was the first country to ban the slave trade.

- From 1792 to 1815, Napoleon Bonaparte rose in power to lead the French army. In 1796 he conquered much of Italy, and in 1798 he defeated Egypt.

- Louis XVI came to the throne of France in 1774. Along with Marie Antoinette, his irresponsible and extravagant queen, he led France to bankruptcy in 1787.

- About one million people died during a six-year famine in Japan from 1780 to 1786. In 1786 the famine was followed by rice riots.

- During the reign of terror in France from 1793 to 1794, a new group known as the Jacobins seized power under the leadership of Robespierre. They beheaded 40,000 people in one year.

- In 1794 the Qaja Dynasty in Persia was founded by Aga Muhammad and lasted for the next 130 years.

- The first fleet of European settlers arrived in Botany Bay, Australia. Most of these settlers were prisoners.

- A vaccination for smallpox was discovered by English doctor Edward Jenner in 1796.

- Now known as Sri Lanka, the country of Ceylon was conquered by the British in 1796.

- The German composer, Ludwig Van Beethoven, was just 17 in the year 1787. He became deaf at the end of his life yet still continued to write music.

- In 1789, the angry citizens of Paris revolted against high taxes and their extravagant king, beginning the French Revolution.

- Toussaint l'Ouverture, a black slave, led a revolt in Haiti and became governor of this island country.

Which Came First?

Work with a partner. Read the following pairs and determine which came first. Circle the appropriate answer.

1.	the Continental Congress	or	the Constitutional Convention
2.	the War of 1812	or	the Revolutionary War
3.	James Madison	or	Ben Franklin
4.	ratification by Rhode Island	or	ratification by New Hampshire
5.	Constitution	or	Articles of Confederation
6.	Whisky Rebellion	or	Shay's Rebellion
7.	Federalists	or	Republican Party
8.	Louisiana Purchase	or	Treaty of Ghent
9.	Great Compromise	or	Virginia Plan
10.	Capitol in Washington, D.C.	or	Capitol in Philadelphia
11.	Bill of Rights	or	Constitution
12.	ratification by New York	or	ratification by North Carolina
13.	Preamble	or	Virginia Plan
14.	U.S. gains freedom from England	or	U.S. becomes a nation
15.	the Federalist Papers	or	Bill of Rights
16.	Declaration of Independence	or	Constitutional Convention
17.	"Star-Spangled Banner"	or	"Yankee Doodle"
18.	Sedition Act	or	Embargo Act

Looking at Art

Three different art projects are discussed below. All are appropriate for use during the study of the Constitution. Incorporate them into your lesson plans where they best suit your purposes.

1. **Artwork of the 1700s.** Direct the students to find books in the library which highlight art from the era. One good resource is *American History in Art* by Rena Newmann Coen (Lerner Publications Company, 1967). With the whole class, brainstorm and list some of the elements of the paintings of that time. For example, which pictures look posed, which are done with oils, etc.

   Materials: drawing paper, pencil

   Directions:
   - Pair the students. One is the artist; the other acts as the subject.
   - Tell the artists to pose their subjects and draw a sketch of them.
   - Reverse roles. Share the pictures.

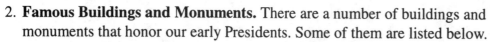

2. **Famous Buildings and Monuments.** There are a number of buildings and monuments that honor our early Presidents. Some of them are listed below.
   - The Jefferson Memorial is a white, marble-domed circular building that houses a nineteen-foot bronze statue of Thomas Jefferson.
   - The Washington Monument in Washington, D.C., is as tall as a 46-story building. It pays tribute to George Washington.
   - Mt. Rushmore in South Dakota honors four Presidents including Washington, Jefferson, Lincoln, and Theodore Roosevelt.

   Materials: clay, papier mâché, cardboard boxes and tubes, empty milk cartons, any other materials that might be useful

   Directions:
   - Instruct the students to find pictures of these and other buildings that honor our early Presidents.
   - Have students draw sketches of their projects and label the materials they will use for each part. (This will act as a "blueprint.")
   - Have them build three-dimensional models using their plans.
   - For a real challenge, tell the students to trade designs with another student and build that person's proposed monument.

3. **Fashions.** Assign students to find out what fashions were in style then. (Men wore powdered wigs; fashionable women wore Empire style dresses,, etc.) Tell them that they are going to create an article of clothing in the 1700s style with a 1900s twist.

   Materials: scraps of fabric; liquid glue; trims; cotton balls; tagboard or other heavy paper; scissors; pencils

   Directions:
   - With pencil, lightly sketch a design on the tagboard.
   - Cut out fabrics and trims to the shape desired.
   - Arrange them on the pencil outline.
   - Glue into place.
   - Have a fashion show where everyone takes turns presenting his or her design.

74

Old-Fashioned Cooking

During the 1700s most foods were cooked on open hearths. Stoves would not become available for another 100 years. Here are three easy recipes that can be cooked over an open fire or barbecue (or even on a stove if a barbecue is not available). Although these are typical foods enjoyed during that era, these recipes have been modernized somewhat.

Apple Pie

    Ingredients: apples, prerolled pie crusts, sugar, cinnamon

    Utensils: paring knife; twig, dowel, or skewer; cup; spoon; waxed paper; aluminum foil

    Directions:

- In a cup, mix 4 tablespoons (60 ml) cinnamon with 1/2 cup (125 ml) sugar; set aside.
- Peel the apples; cut into fourths.
- Roll the apple pieces into the cinnamon sugar.
- Skewer each piece of apple onto a twig or dowel.
- With clean hands press the pie crust into a thin sheet.
- Wrap the crust around the apple.
- Wrap the pie with foil and place on metal racks over an open fire or a barbecue.
- Turn frequently for even cooking.
- Cooking time will vary. Eat the pies from the stick.

        Squaw Corn

        Ingredients: 16 oz. (500 ml) can of whole kernel corn; 4 slices bacon; 1 small onion; salt to taste (makes 4 servings)

        Utensils: Knife, can opener, heavy frying pan with cover

        Directions:

- Chop the onions; drain the corn. Reserve both.
- Cut the bacon into 1-inch (2.5 cm) pieces; place in bottom of pan.
- Spread the onions and the corn on top of the bacon.
- Sprinkle with salt. Cover and cook about 30 minutes.

Quick Cornbread

    Ingredients: 11.5-oz. (322 g.)cans of refrigerated cornbread twists

    Utensils: peeled green stick or a skewer

    Directions:

- Separate the dough twists.
- Starting at the top of the stick wind the dough around the stick. Pinch the dough at each end to hold it in place.
- Cook it over hot coals; turn it frequently. Peel the cornbread away from the stick when it is done.

Extensions:

- Find recipe books that feature foods from colonial times. Have each student choose one recipe and copy it for a class cookbook.
- Assign the students to look for Dolley Madison foods at the grocery store. What types of foods did they find? Why do they think a company might name itself after Dolley Madison?

Freedom of Speech

Develop speaking skills and synthesize knowledge of Constitutional facts with this activity. Cut apart the topics in the boxes below and place them into a specially decorated shoe box or other container. Call on a student to draw a topic and direct him or her to give an answer. Students may stand by their desks or go to the front of the room when speaking. Encourage students to use complete sentences throughout their explanations. You may want to add your own questions to the topic list.

1. In your opinion, was the Grand Convention a success? Defend your answer.

2. The Constitution is sometimes called a miracle. Explain why you think this is a fitting term.

3. If you had been a delegate to the Convention, would you have been for or against a strong central government? Defend your answer.

4. The Constitution was written in secret. Tell why you do or do not think it should have been done this way.

5. Choose a delegate and describe his outstanding characteristics and contributions to the proceedings.

6. Women and slaves were not allowed to vote during this era. Tell when and how each group finally got the vote.

7. If you could have been a delegate, who would you have chosen to be and why?

8. Explain how the meetings of the Constitutional Convention might have been different if women and slaves had been allowed to participate.

9. The delegates worked under some adverse conditions. Which condition do you think was the hardest for them to endure?

10. What if a Bill of Rights had not been added to the Constitution? How do you think it would have affected your rights today?

11. The delegates argued and debated about many issues. Which issue caused the most disagreements; why?

12. Tell why you think the delegates invented the idea of a Supreme Court; explain its purpose.

13. What is the difference between the requirements for candidates to the Senate and candidates to the House of Representatives?

14. James Madison is often called the "Father of the Constitution." Tell why you think he deserves this title.

15. Ben Franklin told a friend he hoped the Constitution would last but that "...nothing is certain but death and taxes." Explain this quote.

Bulletin Boards

Create a Constitutional bulletin board with any of these easy ideas. Some projects may even be suitable for students.

1. **The Preamble.** Line a bulletin board background with stripes of red, white, and blue butcher paper or construction paper. Make a copy of the Preamble (page 28) and glue it to the inside lid of an appropriate-sized box for an instant frame. Attach the Preamble to the center of the bulletin board. Surround it with student-made copies of the paragraph. (See #3 on page 26 for a related activity.)

2. **Graffiti.** Cover the classroom door with butcher paper. Assign students to make a patriotic border of stars and stripes or other appropriate symbols. The door can then be used as a graffiti board. Tell students that this is a covered window in the Philadelphia State House. Have them write statements about the Constitutional proceedings as if they were one of the city's residents. For example, "No kings for us!" or "We demand to know what is transpiring."

3. **Hornbook Lessons.** Cover a bulletin board background with red or blue paper. Create a border with intertwined red, white, and blue crepe paper. Make a copy of the hornbook pattern found on page 13 for each student. Direct them to complete a handwriting assignment or a Constitutional studies-related lesson onto the form. Attach the cut-out hornbook shapes to the bulletin board. Make a title for the board out of a strip of white tagboard or construction paper. It could say "Constitutional Lessons," for example.

4. **On the Ropes.** A rope can be used to make an interesting three-dimensional bulletin board. In a corner or other safe area of the classroom, suspend a rope (or twine or craft yarn) from the floor to the ceiling. Decide on a theme such as a "Timeline of Events that Led to the Constitution." After deciding on the events which you wish to focus on, write them on separate sheets of construction paper. Along with the title, include a paragraph explaining the significance of the event. Arrange the events in chronological order on the rope from top to bottom. Attach the events to the rope with clothespins. (You may want to assign different events to each student pair or group. Have them include pictures, diagrams, or drawings.)

5. **Appliance Boxes.** Cut open a large appliance box to use as a bulletin board. Paint one section red, the next white, the next blue, etc., until all sections have been covered. When the sections are dry, stand the box up. Assign a different topic to each section and make appropriate headings for each one. For example, one section might be used for Current Events, another for Terms to Know, another for displaying student work. Add to the sections throughout the unit. (Appliance boxes can also be use for the mini museum culminating activity found on page 58.)

Award

Let it be known

that on this _____ day of _____

in the year _____

_____

(Student's Name)

has successfully completed a unit of
Constitutional Studies.

Let it further be known that

_____

(Student's Name)

has shown particular interest and promise in the following area(s):

_____

_____

_____

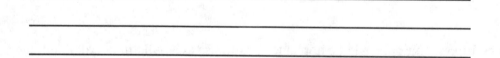

It is with great honor that this certificate is hereby awarded.

Sincerely yours,

_____

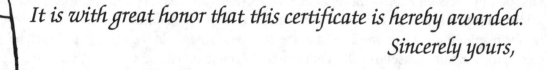

(Teacher's Signature)

78

Bibliography

Historical Literature

Chute, Margaret. *The Green Tree of Democracy.* Dutton, 1971.

Colman, Warren. *The Bill of Rights.* Childrens Press, 1987.

Fisher, Aileen and Oliver Rabe. *Human Rights Day.* Thomas Y. Crowell, 1966.

Fisher, Dorothy Canfield. *Our Independence and the Constitution.* Random House, 1964.

Fritz, Jean. *The Great Little Madison.* G.P. Putnam's Sons, 1989

_____. *Shh! We're Writing the Constitution.* G.P. Putnam's Sons, 1987.

Hauptley, Denis J. *A Convention of Delegates.* Atheneum, 1987.

Hoobler, Dorothy and Thomas Hoobler. *Your Right to Privacy.* Franklin Watts, 1986.

Levy, Elizabeth. *If You Were There When They Signed the Constitution.* Scholastic, 1987.

Mabie, Margot C.J. *The Constitution.* Henry Holt and Company, 1987.

Maestro, Betsy and Giulio. *A More Perfect Union: The Story of Our Constitution.* Lothrop, Lee & Shepard, 1987.

McPhillips, Martin. *The Constitutional Convention.* Silver Burdett, 1985.

Meltzer, Milton. *The Bill of Rights.* Thomas Y. Crowell, 1990.

Morris, Richard B. *The Constitution.* Lerner Publications Company, 1985.

Peterson, Helen Stone. *The Making of the United States Constitution.* Garrard, 1974.

Press, Byron and David Osterlund, editors. *The Constitution of the United States of America. The Bicentennial Keepsake Edition.* Bantam, 1987.

Ritchie, Donald A. *The U.S. Constitution.* Chelsea House, 1989.

Sgroi, Peter. *The Living Constitution. Landmark Supreme Court Decisions.* Julian Messner, 1987.

_____. *...this Constitution.* Franklin Watts, 1986.

Spier, Peter. *We the People: The Constitution of the United States of America.* Doubleday, 1987.

Williams, Selma R. *Fifty-Five Fathers.* Dodd, Mead and Company, 1970.

Periodicals

Cobblestone. "Benjamin Franklin," September, 1992.

"Our Bill of Rights," September, 1991.

"Thomas Jefferson," September, 1989.

"Alexander Hamilton," March, 1987.

"Celebrating Our Constitution, September, 1987.

"The Constitution of the United States," September, 1982.

Instructor July/August, 1993. (Contains information about Constitution Week in September and available learning materials. See page 103 of that issue.)

Multimedia

The Bill of Rights: Evolution of Personal Liberties. Write to Social Studies School Service, 10200 Jefferson Blvd., Room AP, P.O. Box 802, Culver City, CA 90232-0802 (Reproductions of charts, documents, photographs).

The U.S. Constitution Then and Now. Scholastic Software, Scholastic, Inc., 2931 E. McCarty Street, P.O. Box 7502, Jefferson City, MO 65102-9968 (AppleWorks activity package).

Teacher Created Materials

#137 *Newspaper Reporters*

#138 *Newspapers*

#480 *American History Simulations*

#501 *Write All About It*

Answer Key

page 14
1. Alexander Hamilton
2. Ben Franklin
3. Gouverneur Morris
4. John Dickinson
5. Edmund Randolph
6. George Washington
7. James Madison
8. Jacob Shallus
9. Elbridge Gerry
10. Luther Martin

page 16
1. 55 x 13 = 715
2. 1787 + 1777 = 3564
3. 7 x 81 = 567
4. 1774 ÷ 2 = 887
5. 1788 - 1776 = 12
6. 1789 x 4 = 7156
7. 9 x 62 = 558
8. 1790 ÷ 10 = 179
9. 17,000 - 450 = 16,550
10. 1788 x 3 = 5364
11. 1786 + 1808 = 3594
12. 1788 - 28 = 1760

page 19
1. First Continental Congress
2. legislature
3. Articles of Confederation
4. Washington
5. representatives
6. Grand Convention
7. government
8. delegates
9. President
10. proceedings
11. sentries
12. Virginia Plan
13. judicial
14. Congress
15. Great Compromise
16. Constitution

page 20

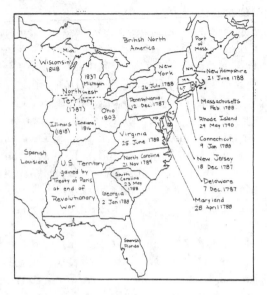

page 36
1. S	2. H	3. S,H	4. H
5. H	6. S,H	7. S	8. S
9. S	10. S,H	11. H	12. H
13. S,H	14. S	15. H	16. S
17. S	18. S,H		

page 38

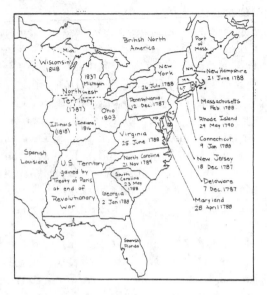

page 39
1. 1,000,000	2. 26	3. 100	4. 6
5. 5	6. 19	7. 500	8. 1937
9. 161	10. 85	11. 2	12. 43
13. 9	14. 15	Challenge: Jacob Shallus	

page 53
Both Liked: experimenting with science; talking about history; a vision of a strong, united republic; reading; planting trees; collecting books; serving their country; corresponding; newfangled gadgets

Both Didn't Like: slavery, Great Britain; Patrick Henry, the lopsided Virginia Constitution, entering into a war

page 55
Both Jefferson and Madison were criticized over the same policy while in office. The 1807 Embargo Act was unpopular and an obvious failure. England was ready to repeal all trade restrictions in 1809 but Madison reminded King George about the Chesapeake incident. Furious, King George called off the agreement.

page 73
1. Continental Congress
2. Revolutionary War
3. Ben Franklin
4. New Hampshire
5. Articles of Confederation
6. Shay's Rebellion
7. Federalists
8. Louisiana Purchase
9. Virginia Plan
10. Capitol in Philadelphia
11. Constitution
12. New York
13. Virginia Plan
14. U.S. gains freedom from England
15. the Federalist Papers
16. Declaration of Independence
17. "Yankee Doodle"
18. Sedition Act